W9-BTJ-907

KANT'S THEORY OF KNOWLEDGE

KANT'S *Theory of Knowledge*

JUSTUS HARTNACK

TRANSLATED BY

M. HOLMES HARTSHORNE

AN ORIGINAL HARBINGER BOOK

HARCOURT, BRACE & WORLD, INC.

NEW YORK

First published in Denmark under the title Kants Erkendelsesteori.
This edition published by arrangement with Gyldendalske Boghandel, Copenhagen.
First edition
Library of Congress Catalog Card Number: 67–22391
Printed in the United States of America

The author and publisher wish to thank Macmillan & Co., Ltd., Macmillan Company of Canada, Ltd., and St. Martin's Press, Inc., for permission to use selections from Norman Kemp Smith's translation of Kant's The Critique of Pure Reason *(London: Macmillan & Co., Ltd., 1929; New York: St. Martin's Press, Inc., 1965) in the footnotes throughout this volume.*

The selection that appears in the footnote on pages 74–75 is reprinted by permission of the publisher from Robert Paul Wolff, Kant's Theory of Mental Activity *(Cambridge, Mass.: Harvard University Press). Copyright, 1963, by the President and Fellows of Harvard College. The selection that appears in the footnote on pages 113–14 is reprinted by permission of the publisher from Gabriele Rabel,* Kant *(Oxford: The Clarendon Press, 1963).*

Acknowledgments

I am grateful to Professor Milton Munitz, New York University, for having read the manuscript of this translation. He has saved me from more than one error. I am particularly grateful to Professor M. Holmes Hartshorne, Colgate University, for the skill, time, and energy he has devoted to the tedious and difficult task of rendering the book from Danish into English.

Justus Hartnack

Contents

KANT'S THEORY OF KNOWLEDGE

1) *Introduction*

Kant is one of the greatest philosophers mankind has produced. He occupies the same distinguished place in the history of modern philosophy that Plato and Aristotle occupy in Greek philosophy. And just as a study of Greek philosophy must necessarily have its center in a study of the works of Plato and Aristotle, so any study of the history of modern philosophy must have its center in a study of Kant. An investigation of Leibniz or Hume is first set in right perspective if it is complemented by a study of Kant. And no one acquainted with post-Kantian philosophy can deny the significance that an understanding of Kant has for an understanding of much of this philosophy.

The significance of Kant's philosophy is to be found primarily in his theory of knowledge, a theory that is set forth in his voluminous work, *The Critique of Pure Reason.* This work, whose first edition saw the light of day in 1781 and whose second edition appeared ("here and there improved," [1] to use Kant's own words) in 1787, is not only voluminous and momentous; it is in addition extraordinarily difficult. Its difficulty is due not only to the fact that the thoughts expressed in it are difficult but also, and not least, to the fact that Kant, after twelve years of intensive thought about the problems, was eager to get them down quickly. According to his own statement he took but four to five months to write out the first edition's 856 pages.[2] No wonder that the reading of this book, so centrally important in the history of philosophy, has given rise to perplexities and made commentaries necessary.

Immanuel Kant was born in Königsberg in 1724, the son of a saddle maker. He was a student in Königsberg, he taught and was University Professor in Königsberg, and in 1804 he died in Königsberg. When his great work on the theory of knowledge was published, he was fifty-seven years old. With this work a long philosophical development came to completion. It is justifiable to speak here of a development, for Kant had worked for many years with the problems of *The Critique of Pure Reason*, and the solution he believed he had found was not identical with that to which he had come in earlier writings. But the thoughts in *The Critique of Pure Reason* are definitive for Kant's position; they are subsequently neither renounced nor modified by him but constitute the basis on which all his later philosophy is built.

[1] This is found on the title page: "Zweite hin und wieder verbesserte Auflage."

[2] In a letter to Moses Mendelssohn (of August 16, 1783) Kant writes: "I had to bring together the result of my thinking of at least twelve years within from four to five months and so to speak do it without a stop. Admittedly, it was done with greatest attention paid to the content but with little labor on the style and of the easing of the reader's insight."

In *The Critique of Pure Reason* Kant attempts, among other things, to establish both the validity of knowledge and the impossibility of metaphysics. His attempt to establish the validity of knowledge is oriented at the outset toward David Hume, whose form of empiricism led with logical necessity to skepticism. Kant's general view of the theory of knowledge, with which the following pages deal, is an attempt to overcome Hume's skepticism. It is at the same time a position that implies the invalidity of all metaphysics, for it excludes the possibility of knowledge without sense experience.

The form of empiricism embraced by Hume, which leads to the invalidity of knowledge—the form of empiricism that Kant opposed—can be explained as follows:

When we observe anything, we do so by means of sense organs. Every one of our sense organs provides us, when they are influenced externally, with sense impressions. On this point Kant and Hume were in agreement. But here their agreement ends. According to Hume observation consists in receiving sense impressions and nothing more. For Kant observation is something other than and more than merely the reception of sense impressions.

Let us suppose that I am looking at a game of billiards. I see one billiard ball roll toward and hit a second billiard ball, which thereafter, as a consequence of the impact it receives, also begins to roll. This is a report of what I see. And yet is it really that? Let us take a second example. I look out of the window, and what do I see? I see a landscape. The word 'landscape,' however, covers here a multitude of things. It must certainly be possible to ask what sort of landscape it is. Let us say that I see green fields, a village and some white houses with thatched roofs, and trees. But what I call seeing a tree is seeing a trunk, foliage, leaves, branches, and twigs; and what I call seeing a house is (in this case) seeing a white wall, some rectangular panes of glass, chimneys, and much else. And if I further describe what I see when I say that I see these things—describe that which immediately exists as sense impression, i.e., describe that and only that which exists for my senses—then the description will be solely in the form of colors and figures.

A further example. I eat an orange. An exact description of all that I sense in such a situation includes a certain perception of temperature in my fingers as they hold the orange, and a certain perception of temperature caused by the piece of orange that I have put in my mouth. In addition there is the particular perception of solidity that I have in holding the orange. There exist also different colors, taste impressions, and smells. All these different impressions constitute the sensory content in the given situation. They are what sensation provides us with.

If one now supposes, as did Hume, that we must restrict ourselves to what sensation provides us with, to hold to that which is given in sensation, then we are led, just as Hume was led, to deny the validity of much that we actually cannot avoid assuming—a fact that Hume was the first to emphasize. Let me only mention two such things.

We say that we see something or other, for example, an orange, but we say also that we see this thing's qualities. I see the orange, and I see also that it is orange in color. I see that the orange has certain properties. We distinguish, and we think that we necessarily must distinguish, between a thing and its properties. But what shall we understand by that which we call the 'thing'? If one is an empiricist of the Humean variety, then one is not entitled to understand by it anything other than what sense impressions entitle one to; and sense impressions are various colors, taste impressions, smells, etc.—i.e., that, and only that, which is included under the concept 'property.' In other words a thing is nothing other than the sum of its properties. But such a view leads to conceptual difficulties.

In the first place, one cannot say that a thing consists of or is the sum of its properties. The orange does not consist of nor is it the sum of an orange color, a sweet taste, and a perception of a certain kind of texture. We do not find certain entities called properties, which we can then put together and thereby get a thing. That this is so is not an empirical but a logical truth. Further, it is not an empirical but rather a logical truth that a color must always be a thing that is colored, and that a taste always must be a thing that has taste. The Humean form of empiricism implies, therefore, not only that one must maintain that a thing is nothing else than the sum of its properties; it implies in addition that one no longer has the right to use the term 'property.' It is nonsense to speak of a property that is not a property of something.

Another difficulty is this. If a thing changes, nevertheless we conceive of it as being one and the same thing. A piece of wax, which has, after being warmed, another temperature, another smell, and another color, continues nonetheless to be one and the same piece of wax. But we could not maintain that it was the same wax if we were also to maintain that a thing is the sum of its properties. For the properties are not the same as before, yet the thing is the same thing. To admit the Humean form of empiricism seems, in other words, to lead to a collapse of the concepts we employ in our view of the external world.

Let us return to the example of the billiard ball, which by striking the second billiard ball makes this second ball roll. What is meant by saying that the one ball *makes* the second roll? The expression 'makes' means here the same thing as 'causes,' 'brings about,' 'leads to,' and one could use other similar phrases. We distinguish, and we think that we necessarily must distinguish, between an event being caused by (a consequence of, following as a result of) another event, and an event merely following temporally after another. The second ball in our illustration begins to roll not only *after* it is hit by the first; it begins to roll also *because of* this.

A bus punctually passes a church every morning just before the church clock strikes eight. The church clock always begins to strike immediately after the bus passes it, but it does not strike the hour as a consequence of this.

Humean empiricism, however, does not justify such a distinction. No sense impression exists that can show us the difference between merely following after another event temporally and following as a consequence of the event. In other words: to follow as a consequence of is not, according to Hume, something that is essentially different from merely following after. It means simply that one is accustomed to seeing a certain kind of event succeeded always by a certain other kind of event, whereby one is led to the view that this is something that necessarily must happen. The difference between saying that something happens as a result of something else and that something happens after something else, does not, according to Hume, lie in the fact that there is an inner bond that joins them or that there is a discernible power which produces the effect, but simply in the fact that this particular sequence of events seems always to have been the case. The concept 'because of' is defined by means of the concept 'temporal succession.'

But if this be right—and it is a necessary consequence of Humean empiricism—then we find ourselves without any answer to the question as to how one knows that things will continue to happen in the way they always have happened. How can the fact that something has heretofore been the case constitute a guarantee that it will continue to be the case? That something heretofore has occurred in a particular way does not give us grounds for supposing that it will continue to do so. Humean empiricism has therefore disastrous consequences for our view and understanding of reality.

On the whole, we conceive of a thing as a thing that has different properties; i.e., we make a distinction between the properties (color, smell, shape, taste, etc.) and the thing that has the properties. Our concept of a thing is therefore not identical with the concept of the sum of its properties. And generally we think of a cause as something *causing* its effect and not merely preceding it in time. We therefore assume that we can predict what effect a given cause necessarily will have—a conclusion that, among other things, is a necessary presupposition of that knowledge on the basis of which we carry on our daily affairs.

But according to Humean empiricism these assumptions are unwarranted. They are unwarranted in the sense that no ground can be found for them. They are not, however, unwarranted in the sense that we are doomed to disappointment if and when we act on them; on the contrary, we are actually never disappointed. But we must, according to Hume, understand that from a logical standpoint we ought to be surprised that we are never disappointed. Psychologically speaking we have become accustomed to these assumptions. Through constant repetition we have become fooled into believing that there is a necessity where actually none exists—fooled into believing that there are rational and logical grounds where there are none.

The result of Humean empiricism, the result of thinking that knowledge builds upon and contains nothing other than that which is given in sense experience, is consequently a denial of knowledge and the collapse of those concepts we necessarily must employ in order to speak about and to understand reality. If Humean empiricism is true, then there is no knowledge. And conversely, if there is knowledge, then Humean empiricism is false.

Faced with these alternatives Kant thinks that Hume must be opposed. In other words, Kant maintains that there is knowledge and that Humean empiricism must therefore be false. To assert that Humean empiricism is false is to assert that knowledge does not simply consist in receiving sense impressions. Or more correctly, sense impressions, in order to be sense impressions at all, must be subject to certain conditions. If these conditions were not fulfilled, no sense impressions could be perceived by us. These conditions are universally valid and necessary. They are of two kinds. First, there are the conditions under which a sense impression can be a sense impression at all, and second, the conditions under which a single sense impression can exist not simply as a sense impression, but as a sense impression that is bound together with other sense impressions—bound together so that what appears is judged to be not a bundle of sense impressions but a thing, or is judged not as two events that merely follow temporally one after the other, but as events that are connected in such fashion that the one event is viewed as the effect of the other.

But how do we arrive at these conditions? That one cannot discover them through the simple reception of sense impressions follows already from their status as *conditions* of sense impressions. The conditions of there being any sense impressions at all certainly cannot themselves exist as sense impressions. The conditions are what Kant calls *a priori,* i.e., conditions that viewed logically are prior to sensation.

A judgment can be about what is given through the senses, and whether it is true or false is decided through experience. "The woods are green" is an example of such judgment. It is only after we have ascertained through observation that the woods are in fact green that we know the judgment to be true. Apart from any observation at all we could not have known that the woods were green. However, there is another kind of judgment that is characterized by just such independence of observation. That all bachelors are unmarried, that all four-footed animals are animals and that the sum of the interior angles of a triangle is 180 degrees, are judgments whose truth is not determined by interrogating each and every bachelor, examining every four-footed animal, and measuring the sum of the angles in each and every triangle. These judgments are necessarily true. On the other hand, they do not tell us anything that we do not already know.

Let us further clarify the difference between these two kinds of judgment. Since the time of Aristotle it has been customary to consider a judgment as consisting of a subject and a predicate. The subject of a judgment is that about which the judgment affirms something, and the predicate is that which is predicated of the subject. In the judgment, "The woods are green," the subject is 'the woods' (it is the woods about which something is affirmed, namely that they are green) and the predicate is 'green' (what is said of the subject is that it is green). If we now compare the two judgments, (1) "The woods are green" and (2) "All bachelors are unmarried," we can express the difference between them as follows: (1) the predicate 'green' affirms something that is not already contained in the concept of the subject. There is nothing in the concept 'woods' that makes it necessary that the property 'green' be predicated of it. It would not be a logical contradiction to deny that the woods are green. With (2) it is otherwise. Here the predicate does not predicate anything other than that which is already contained in the concept 'bachelor.' If one knows what the concept 'bachelor' means then one also knows that the predicate 'to be unmarried' must necessarily be affirmed of it. We know that it would be a contradiction to deny that all bachelors are unmarried.

A judgment in which the predicate is not contained in the concept of the subject Kant called 'synthetic,' while a judgment in which the predicate is already contained in the concept of the subject was called 'analytic.' The judgment that the woods are green is therefore a synthetic judgment, while the judgment that all bachelors are unmarried is an analytic judgment. Since the truth value of synthetic judgments is first known through experience, these are judgments of experience, or to use another expression for the same thing, empirical judgments. Kant calls such judgments 'synthetic *a posteriori*.' Analytic judgments, whose truth value is independent of experience, are therefore judgments that are a priori. We have thus these two kinds of judgments:

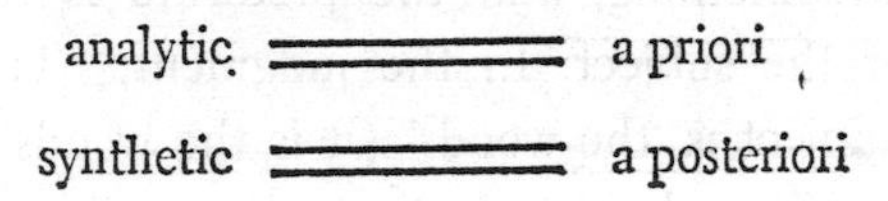

Hume recognizes this classification of judgments. Furthermore, Hume and Kant are in agreement that analytic judgments do not give us any knowledge of reality. They are only expressions for an analysis of the concept of the subject. Hume and Kant are also in agreement about the existence of synthetic a posteriori judgments. According to Hume it is these judgments that deal with (and deal with nothing else than) that with which our senses provide us.

There is, however, the possibility of a third kind of judgment, namely judgments which are both synthetic and a priori —that is to say, judgments where the predicate states something about the subject that is not already contained in the concept of the subject of the judgment, and where that which is predicated is nevertheless necessarily true, is necessary and universally valid. The three types of judgments that, according to Kant, can be made are then these:

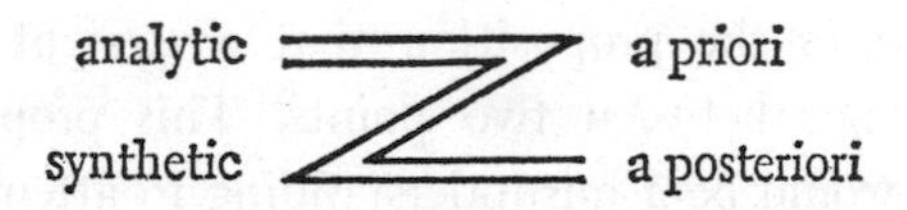

By maintaining that there are synthetic a priori judgments Kant maintains *ipso facto* that knowledge cannot consist exclusively in the receiving of sense impressions. For any judgment that is a report about sense impressions we have received (i.e., an empirical judgment, or a judgment of experience) can only be synthetic a posteriori and can therefore never be universally valid and necessarily true. So in case there are judgments that at one and the same time are both synthetic and a priori, it follows, as Kant says, that even if knowledge begins with sense experience it does not stem exclusively from it. Or to put it another way, even if sense experience is a necessary condition of knowledge, it is not a sufficient condition.

Among those judgments that are synthetic a priori are, according to Kant, mathematical judgments. As an example Kant gives the proposition that $7 + 5 = 12$. It is a priori (i.e., universally valid and necessary and therefore independent of verification by experience), for if a man knows that he had seven items and knows also that he has just got five more, then he does not need to count them in order to assure himself that he now has twelve in all. If he were afterwards to count them and come to a result other than twelve, no one would take this as proof that 7 + 5 are not after all (or in any case not always) 12, but that there were not seven to begin with, or that he did not in fact get five other items but some other number instead, or that he had counted incorrectly. Moreover, this judgment is synthetic, for the predicate '12' is not contained in the subject '7 + 5.' This latter concept contains only the notion that these two numbers shall be added but contains nothing as to what the result is. As a further illustration of this point Kant cites the proposition that a straight line is the shortest distance between two points. This proposition is a priori, for it would be a misunderstanding to attempt to verify it by measuring; we know that the proposition is correct independently of any possible measurements. If by measuring we were to discover that it is not the shortest distance, we would not take this as evidence that we had discovered an instance where a straight line is not the shortest distance. We would regard it as evidence either that we had not measured correctly in the first place or that it was, after all, not a straight line. And the judgment is synthetic, because the concept 'straight' does not contain anything about distance.

Kant further thinks that the principles of natural science contain synthetic a priori judgments. The two examples he mentions are the principle of the constancy of the quantity of matter and the principle that the force that one body exerts on another is equal to the force that the second body exerts on the first.

These two examples are from mathematics and physics. Is it also possible to pass such judgments in metaphysics? By metaphysics one can understand (and indeed has understood) many different things. In some cases the word 'metaphysics' means a significant, interesting and necessary discipline.

In other instances the word can signify a discipline whose justification is arguable and has often been denied. Where the word connotes a meaningful and necessary discipline, metaphysics is a logical examination of the fundamental concepts by means of which we grasp and understand reality (and is therefore also an examination of the language we employ in our thinking and speaking about reality). Where metaphysics signifies a discipline whose justification is argued and often denied, it means an examination of reality, but one, be it noted, resulting in assertions about reality that it is in principle impossible, by any form of experience, either to verify or to falsify. In other words, this form of metaphysics entails assertions about something beyond experience, which at the same time employ concepts whose significance is, in the last analysis, borrowed from the realm of experience, in consequence of which justification for their being used outside of this realm can be called into question. It is this last meaning of the word that Kant employs when he attempts to examine whether or not we are entitled to make judgments in metaphysics that are both synthetic and a priori. If we make judgments in metaphysics (in this last meaning of the word), they must necessarily be synthetic, otherwise they would not be assertions that extended our knowledge of reality; and they must also be a priori, for were they a posteriori they would be simply judgments of experience. Among such metaphysical assertions Kant includes assertions about God's existence, the freedom of the will, and the immortality of the soul.

With respect to metaphysics Kant notes that it is one thing to recognize that reason, by virtue of its own inner logic, is unavoidably led to pose metaphysical questions and to set forth metaphysical assertions as answers to these questions; it is a quite different thing to investigate whether these questions are justified, i.e., whether there are assertions that not only are synthetic but are also a priori (which would be the same as saying that they are universally valid and necessarily true).

We have thus reached this point: it is a fact (Kant believes) that synthetic a priori judgments are found in mathematics and physics. It is likewise a fact that reason by virtue of its own inner logic is led to propound metaphysical propositions. Setting out from these facts, Kant formulates his basic problem as follows: How are synthetic a priori judgments possible? To answer this question is also to answer the following questions:

1. How are synthetic judgments in mathematics possible?
2. How are synthetic a priori judgments in physics possible?
3. How are synthetic a priori judgments in metaphysics possible?

The third question is, as we have seen, actually two questions. There is first the question: How are these supposed synthetic a priori judgments in metaphysics possible? This is a question about how the metaphysical questions follow the nature of human reason itself. The second question is this: Are synthetic a priori judgments in metaphysics possible?

The question of how synthetic a priori judgments are possible, it should be understood, does not ask what psychological capacities men have that enable them to make such judgments but how we can know that such judgments are valid.

The first question is answered in the *Transcendental Aesthetic*, the second question is answered in the *Transcendental Analytic*, and the third is answered in the *Transcendental Dialectic*.

2) The Transcendental Aesthetic

In the Transcendental Aesthetic Kant sets out to answer the question as to how it is possible to make judgments in mathematics that are both synthetic and a priori. The question will have been answered if he can find a principle that constitutes the necessary as well as the sufficient conditions for making such judgments. The answer he comes to is that space and time are a priori forms of intuition.

Kant attempts to show this first with respect to space and next, by parallel arguments, with respect to time.

What is space? Through a four-point analysis Kant seeks to clarify the logical character of space. This is carried out in what he calls the metaphysical exposition of space (*Metaphysiche Erörterung dieses Begriffs*). The four points are as follows:

1. Space is not an empirical concept derived from external experience. What Kant here opposes is so-called abstractionism. According to abstractionism, the logical order of the cognitive process is that man begins by observing things and the properties of things and thereafter forms concepts by abstraction. For example, I observe that several different things are red or, in other words, that several different things share the property 'red.' By ignoring all else I proceed to form the concept 'red.' Thus the presupposition for forming this concept is that I have observed things that are red. Abstractionism, as a philosophical theory, has had but few adherents among philosophers and is today regarded with skepticism. Kant's reason for denying that the concept of space can be formed by abstraction is simply this: space is a necessary presupposition for being able to observe (intuit) at all. I can observe that a thing is always at some particular place, or more correctly, that everything must necessarily be found at some place or other; this is a universally valid and necessary (i.e., a priori) truth. But it would be nonsense to say that space must be found some place or other. This shows the logical difference between the thing that is found in space and the space it is found in. Space neither is nor is not a place; it is rather the necessary condition for the universally valid and necessary truth that things must be found somewhere.

2. Space is a necessary, a priori representation that underlies all outer intuitions. One cannot imagine that there is no space, but one can imagine that there is nothing in this space. In saying that one cannot imagine there is no space, Kant is not here speaking about a psychological 'cannot.' It is not by virtue of some deficiency of our representational powers that we are

unable to imagine (think) space away, something we could perhaps do if we were a different kind of beings. Were Kant's assertion a psychological assertion, it would be one that simply established a fact. It would be an empirical assertion, which consequently would be neither universally valid nor necessarily true. Kant's 'cannot' is of a logical sort. Independent of what kind of psychological structure we might have had, it would have been impossible to think away space; for nothing could count as a representation (*Vorstellung*) where space had been thought away. The assumption that we could have a representation where space is thought away would be meaningless. Kant's 'cannot' is as little a psychological 'cannot' as the 'cannot' in the assertation "One cannot imagine a point without extension" (cf. the psychological assertion: "I cannot imagine [see with my inner eye] how he would look if he were red-haired"). It is not by virtue of a deficiency of imagination that I cannot imagine a point without extension; it is because it is a logical absurdity.

3. Space is not a discursive concept but a pure (i.e., a priori) intuition. We are able to imagine only one space, although we can imagine this one space divided into different segments of various sizes. What is decisive, however, is that these different segments are parts of space precisely in the sense that they are divisions and not constituents of space. Space is not compounded of (in the sense of made up of) different portions of space, but these portions of space necessarily presuppose space. You can make a table by joining together table legs and a table top, but you cannot construct space by piling different portions of space on top of each other or setting them along side of each other. This is a priori impossible, because the

conditions for setting them 'on top of one another' or laying them 'beside each other' already presuppose space; the concepts 'on top of' and 'beside' are themselves spatial concepts.

4. Space is not a concept but an a priori intuition. A concept (in a certain meaning of the word 'concept') can have infinitely many instances. There are, for example, infinitely many cats, and every one of these infinitely many cats is an instance of the concept 'cat.' But no single cat, much less any and all cats, is identical with the concept 'cat.' The concept 'cat' neither walks on four legs nor eats mice. But space is not a concept. We can talk about different segments, divisions or parts of space, but none of these segments or parts are *instances* of space; they are parts of it. There is just as great a logical difference between a form of intuition and a concept as there is between the concept 'a part of' and the concept 'an instance of.' A piece of cake I have cut is precisely a piece of the cake and not an instance of it. The actual cake that I cut into has no instances but is itself an instance, namely an instance of the concept 'cake.' Instances of a concept I can divide and eat; but I can neither divide nor eat the concept.

As this point in the Transcendental Aesthetic Kant thinks that he has proved that space is an a priori form of intuition. He seeks next to show that as an a priori form of intuition space is a necessary and sufficient condition for making judgments in geometry that are synthetic a priori. Such a proof he calls a 'transcendental examination' (*Transcendentale Erörterung des Begriffs vom Raume*).

Geometry, according to Kant, is a synthetic a priori determination of the properties of space, for it is a science (this Kant thinks he has shown) in which we are in a position to make synthetic a priori judgments about just such spatial concepts as straight lines and shortest distances. The condition of making such judgments is that space is a priori; otherwise judgments about the properties of space could not be a priori. But since the metaphysical inquiry (*Die Metaphysiche Erörterung*) has shown that space is a priori, this condition is accordingly fulfilled.

The condition of making judgments about space that are not only a priori but also synthetic is that space is not a concept but a form of intuition. For from a concept one cannot deduce other than what this concept contains; thus merely on the basis of a knowledge of the concept one cannot affirm anything about this concept that is not already contained in it. An a priori intuition is therefore a necessary condition of making synthetic a priori judgments in geometry.

What does Kant mean by saying that one cannot deduce anything from a concept other than that which the concept contains? Some concepts are determined by definition. This is true, for example, of many of the concepts that are introduced into one or another of the sciences. The concept is, so to say, born through definition; it is created through it. The concept's meaning is thus determined by its definition: it means what the definition says it means, and it means this and nothing else. What judgments we are entitled to make about such a concept are determined, therefore, through and by the definition. Things are a bit more complicated, however, in the case of those concepts that cannot be determined by definition—something that is often true of just those concepts that have philosophical significance. What is implied in such concepts as, for example, 'existence' and 'reality' is discovered through a philosophical examination. If it is a concept that can be defined, the definition is a result of such an inquiry and not the point of departure for the inquiry. But here also it seems fair to think that what is arrived at through philosophical inquiry is a clarification of the concept and not an amplification of it. We certainly may arrive at something we had not known before, but we do not arrive at (logically speaking we *cannot* arrive at) other than what the concept contains. If within geometry synthetic judgments can be made that are a priori (and this is precisely what Kant maintains), and if geometry is a discipline about the properties of space (and this too is what Kant affirms), then it follows that space cannot be a concept but must be an intuition.

Kant herewith completes his examination of space. He has shown that it is an a priori form of intuition and that it is a necessary and sufficient condition for making judgments in geometry that are both synthetic and a priori. His next examination is concerned with time, an examination that is carried on in a way that parallels the examination of space.

1. Time is not an empirical concept. We do not get the concept 'time' by abstracting from experience. On the contrary, we cannot experience anything without presupposing time. I observe that two things happen simultaneously or that one thing occurs before another. I would not be in a position to observe this, would not be able to register this observation, did I not already have the idea of time. How could I explain what it means to say that one thing follows after another thing? If the person to whom I must explain it does not already know what time is, the task would seem hopeless. It is no use for me to say that it means that this event comes *first* and the other event comes afterwards, for that is to explain it by means of concepts that are already temporal concepts. Let us suppose that I attempt it in the following way: I begin by saying that I will show it by using my right hand. I ask the person to pay attention to

my right hand, for it is to appear after my left hand. Thereupon I hold up first my left hand and immediately afterwards my right. But this illustration will be instructive only if the person can make the judgment that the right hand came after the left —that is, if he already knows what it means to say that one thing occurs after another. If he does not already know this, he certainly will not learn it from this illustration. Another way of expressing the same point is that the concept 'time' is incapable of being defined, for whatever concept might be used in its definition would always be a concept in which time is presupposed. This is the case, for example, with concepts such as 'change,' 'succession,' and 'progress.' We speak of measuring time, but this ought not to lead us to suppose that time is an empirical process. For no time process exists. There are innumerable processes—biological, physiological, chemical, and hundreds of others—but among these innumerable processes there is none that could be called a time process. It is a universally valid and necessarily true proposition that every event and process occurs at a given moment in time and that every process takes a certain time; but time itself does not occur at a certain point in time and does not itself take a certain time. The presupposition of something taking time does not itself take time.

2. Time is a necessary idea. One cannot imagine a world that is not in time, i.e., a world where nothing happens either before, at the same time as, or after something else. One can, according to Kant, easily imagine that nothing happens and that nothing exists (and therefore that nothing occurs before, at the same time as, or after anything else) but not that there is no time. Time as a constant flow cannot be thought away. The first of these propositions is logically and necessarily true (and so is not a psychological assertion). To maintain that something occurs

is by implication to maintain that it occurs at a certain point in time and that it occurs at the same time as, or after, something else. The second proposition is, however, not completely clear. What is meant by saying that time and nothing but time exists is not obvious. If time presupposes that something occurs before, at the same time as, or after something else, or that something persists, then it would appear that we are entitled no longer to speak of time if it is assumed that there is nothing happening and that nothing exists. If time does not necessarily presuppose that something occurs either before, at the same time as, or after something, or that there is something that endures, then it is hard to see what can be understood by the concept 'time.'

3. Time is not a discursive concept but an a priori intuition. We can speak of different segments and periods of time, but such segments and periods are parts of one and the same time, not its constituents. Time is not constituted by the sum of discrete temporal units; for to add units of time together would mean that one unit of time *follows after* another; but in the concept 'follows after' time is already presupposed.

That we can only add units of time where we view them as following one after another and not existing simultaneously is not only an a priori truth but also, Kant maintains, a synthetic truth. Therefore it cannot be deduced from the *concept* 'time' (compare the corresponding argument in Kant's exposition of space). A synthetic a priori proposition concerning time presupposes that time is not a concept but an a priori *intuition.*

4. If every moment, every period or unit of time, must be considered as a part of time but not that out of which time is formed—that is, that time is not formed by the addition of

these parts—then it follows that every single segment of time must be considered as a limitation of that which these parts or segments of time are parts of. With respect to the logical order, the parts are secondary, the whole is primary. We can no more speak of a segment of time without presupposing that of which it is a segment than we can talk about a half, a third, or a tenth without already having presupposed that of which the half is a half, or the third is a third, or the tenth is a tenth. Time as something unlimited is therefore a necessary presupposition for speaking (in the way we actually do) of what is temporally limited. Likewise single segments of time are not instances of that time of which they are segments (cf. the fourth argument under space). Time is accordingly not a concept but an intuition.

When Kant comes to the transcendental exposition of time, we would expect that he would attempt to prove that time as an a priori intuition is a necessary and sufficient condition for making synthetic a priori judgments in arithmetic. However, only much later in *The Critique of Pure Reason* (on B 182) does he express himself (and then only sketchily) on the relationship between arithmetic and time as an a priori form of intuition. Numbers, Kant maintains, are constructed by the successive addition of units. It is this successive moving forward in time that, just because it is an a priori intuition, determines synthetic a priori judgments respecting numbers.

Under the metaphysical exposition of time four arguments have here been mentioned. Actually there are five arguments, but the third of these five arguments, strictly speaking, does not (as Kant admits) fall within the metaphysical exposition but within the transcendental. This argument is as follows: there are certain fundamental principles concerning time that are universally valid and necessary. Of the principles Kant mentions these: time has only one dimension (it moves in one and only one direction, namely forward), and different points in time can not be simultaneous but must follow after one another. Such principles, which are both synthetic and a priori, cannot be arrived at through experience, for judgments of experience can only be synthetic a posteriori. The necessary and sufficient condition of such synthetic a priori principles is that time is an a priori form of intuition.

The transcendental exposition is based on the conditions of change. Nothing can change (including changing its position in space) without time being a presupposition; change means, as Aristotle had already maintained, that contradictory predicates are predicated of one and the same object. From being red the object becomes something that is not red, from being warm it becomes something that is not warm, from being ten meters long it becomes something that is not ten meters long, etc. The only possibility of predicating contradictory predicates of one and the same object is that these predicates are not predicated simultaneously. A necessary and sufficient condition of change taking place is consequently time as an a priori form of intuition.

In the Transcendental Aesthetic Kant introduces the distinction between what he calls 'things-in-themselves' (*die Dinge an sich*) and things as they appear in intuition (what he calls *Erscheinungen*). The correct interpretation of this distinction is still under discussion.[1] According to one interpretation the relationship is this: intuited things are intuited in space, for this is a condition of their being intuited at all. We can therefore distinguish between two kinds of existences. On the one hand there are things-in-themselves, i.e., things as they exist independ-

[1] The distinction is further elucidated in the fourth paralogism. Cf. p. 108.

ently of intuition. They are therefore not in space; they are not spatial things but a kind of mysterious entity about which nothing can be said and of which nothing can be predicated except two things: they exist, and they are causes of the things we intuit in space. The relationship between these two existences, between the thing-in-itself and the intuited thing (which is the other kind of existence), can be illustrated in the following manner.

Let us suppose that all things lie in darkness and that it is only by being projected on an illuminated radar screen that they can be seen. We have now two kinds of entities: on the one hand things-in-themselves, which never can be intuited since they lie in darkness, and on the other hand pictures on the radar screen, which can be seen, since they fulfill the necessary conditions for being seen, namely to be illuminated. The point of this illustration (which certainly falters in some respects) is threefold: First, just as the unilluminated things cannot be seen, because they have no light, so things-in-themselves can never be known, because they are not in space. Second, just as the thing and the picture of the thing on the radar screen are two different entities, so also the thing-in-itself and the intuited thing are two different entities. Third, there is a similarity between the relation of the thing and the picture on the radar screen, on the one hand, and the relation of the thing-in-itself and the intuited thing, on the other hand: both are causal relationships. The thing is the cause of the picture on the radar screen, and the thing-in-itself is the cause of the intuited thing. A decisive difference, however, is that while the thing and the picture on the radar screen are spatially distinct, it makes no sense, according to Kant, to say that the thing-in-itself and the intuited thing are spatially distinct (whether in that case it makes sense to view them as two different entities is even doubtful!), for the thing-in-itself is not in space. That space is a priori is sometimes understood, according to the interpretation with which we are here dealing, to mean that space has its origin in the subject (Kant says at one place in the Aesthetic that space is "the subjective conditions of sensibility").

But this must not in any case be understood as meaning that space is subjective in the same empirical sense in which we can call different sense perceptions subjective. As the condition of objective intuition, space can no more be said to be subjective than can the illuminated radar screen be said to be subjective; on the contrary, it is the condition of objective intuition. Only that which is intuited in space has what Kant calls objective validity. Space has, therefore, empirical reality, but it is not real in the case of the thing-in-itself. Kant expresses this relation by saying that space has *empirical reality* (*empirische Realität*) but *transcendental ideality* (*transcendentale Idealität*).

However, another interpretation is possible of the distinction between the thing-in-itself and the intuited thing. Instead of the thing-in-itself and the intuited thing being regarded as two different existing entities, the intuited thing is viewed as the only existing thing. Thus there is no question of the intuited thing being caused by the thing-in-itself, nor is there any question of the thing-in-itself being considered as a mystical, existing, unextended thing. The expression 'thing-in-itself' must not, and cannot, signify some form of thing or entity or indeed anything that can be the cause of an intuited thing. For, as Kant shows later on in *The Critique of Pure Reason*, both the concept 'thing' and the concept 'cause' are only useful in the world of intuited things. What does not appear in time and space and is not conceptualized (i.e., is not comprehended by means of concepts) does not, according to Kant, satisfy the necessary conditions of being known. Not only can it not be known or thought (and therefore not be talked about); it cannot even be said to exist. An alleged thing, which is not at any place nor at any point in time and of which, moreover, nothing can be predicated, cannot meaningfully be said to exist. The thing-in-itself as a concept is thus merely an expression for the boundaries of knowledge and hence of thought and meaningful speech.[2] The concept 'thing-in-itself' is not a concept of a special thing that exists yet is unknowable. It is, rather, an underscoring of the fact that things that are not in space are a logical impossibility; for it is a synthetic a priori truth that everything is in space. When Kant speaks of the existence and reality of the outer world, and when he speaks of a causal connection between an external thing and the sense organs, then according to this interpretation, he is speaking of the intuited thing (*Erscheinung*).

There are other possible interpretations than those mentioned here. However, the interpretations all range between (1) psychological interpretations on the one hand, which consider space and therefore also the intuited thing as subjective, and (2) logical and epistemological interpretations on the other, which consider space and the intuited thing as objective and regard it a misunderstanding of Kant's thoughts to conceive of the thing-in-itself as the cause of the intuited thing. What makes it difficult to decide which interpretation is the right one is that Kant, at times, almost in so many words, expresses a psy-

[2] One is reminded here of Russell's doctrine according to which the expression 'existence' or 'exists' can only be predicated of propositional functions; but an alleged propositional function, where it is logically impossible to give any value to the predicate variable, is no propositional function at all. Cf. Bertrand Russell's "The Philosophy of Logical Atomism," Lecture 5, reprinted in Russell's *Logic and Knowledge: Essays 1901–1950*, ed. Robert Charles Marsh (London: Allen & Unwin, 1956; New York: Macmillan). Cf. also Quine, "On What There Is," reprinted in Quine, *From a Logical Point of View* (2nd rev. ed.; Cambridge, Mass.: Harvard University Press, 1961).

chological view, while at other times he explicitly denies such a point of view. The development of Kant research has shown a clear trend away from the psychological interpretation, which earlier was the prevailing one, toward a logical understanding of the theory of knowledge.[3]

Regardless, however, of which interpretation one considers to be correct, be it the subjective and psychological one or not, it can never result in the view that in the Aesthetic Kant has proved that space and time are subjective, i.e., subjective in the sense that space and time stand and fall with the existence of intuiting beings.

If space and time are 'nothing other than' forms of intuition, are we not thereby saying that when there is no intuition and nothing is being intuited, then neither is there space and time? This Kant could never concede, for if space and time are the conditions of all intuition (space of all outer, and time of all outer, as well as of all inner, intuition), then space and time are presupposed by *all* statements concerning reality—thus also by statements asserting that time and space do not exist. And since this is a self-destroying assertion (for it denies the presuppositions upon which it can be set forth) it cannot really be made at all.

[3] One of the strongest attacks upon a psychological view is to be found in the work of the Uppsala philosopher, Hägerström: *Kant's Ethik*, published in 1902. In addition see the works of two other Uppsala philosophers and students of Hägerström: Konrad Marc-Wogau, *Untersuchungen zur Raumlehre Kants* (1931) and Gunnar Oxenstierna, *Psykologiska och Logiska Moment i Kants fornufskritik* (1934). One of the most recent attempts at a consistent, logical, and epistemological view is Graham Bird's *Kant's Theory of Knowledge* (New York. Humanities Press, 1962).

3) The Transcendental Analytic

THE METAPHYSICAL DEDUCTION

The conclusions of the Transcendental Aesthetic are the following:

1. Space and time are a priori forms of intuition.
2. As a priori forms of intuition, space is a necessary condition for all outer intuition and time is a necessary condition for all outer and inner intuition.
3. As a priori form of intuition, space and time are the necessary and sufficient conditions for the synthetic a priori judgments we are able to make in mathematics.

In the Transcendental Analytic Kant sets out to find the conditions for making synthetic a priori judgments in physics.

The Aesthetic elucidates the conditions of intuition. But a simple intuition is not the same as the comprehending of (the thinking about or understanding of) that which is intuited. To intuit is not the same as to make a judgment about what is intuited. The condition of thinking (understanding, making a judgment about, conceiving) that which is intuited is the employment of concepts, and this is an activity of the understanding. For according to Kant, the understanding is the capacity to employ concepts. This must not be understood to mean that *first* one intuits and *then afterwards* one thinks that which has been intuited. An intuition that at the same time is not also a comprehension of the intuited does not exist; to intuit is, also, to have grasped or understood that which is intuited. The employment of the concepts of the understanding presupposes that which is given in intuition. As Kant expresses it: "thoughts without content are empty, and intuition without concepts are blind" (B 75).

The concepts of which we are here speaking are a priori concepts, i.e., concepts that are not formed by abstracting from experience. The concept 'cat' is not an a priori concept but an empirical concept. On the other hand, the concept 'because of' is not an empirical concept. This was exactly what Hume had shown, and it was just for this reason that he denied the validity of the concept 'cause,' which is an a priori concept. It is used in order to understand that which is intuited, but it is not itself intuited. Kant further points out that a priori concepts are used for (are necessary conditions of) making synthetic a priori judgments. The examination of such concepts, an examination embracing their number and nature, their validity, and the conditions of their use, Kant calls *transcendental logic*. Transcendental logic is thus different from ordinary, so-called formal logic. Formal logic abstracts from all empirical content; it is concerned only with the logically consistent conclusions we are entitled to draw by virtue of the logical form of different kinds of propositions. It has nothing to do with the possibility that these propositions have of being used to set forth true assertions. Transcendental logic is concerned with the concepts of the understanding and with the conditions of their employment.

To use a concept is, according to Kant, to make a judgment by means of this concept. Since the understanding is the faculty of using concepts, it can therefore also be said to be the faculty of making judgments. If I say of the animal I am looking at, "This is a cat," then I have used the empirical concept 'cat' in order to make this judgment. What I have intuited is judged by me to be a cat. What exists as mere intuition is simply multicolored shapes (what Hume would call sense impressions), but by means of the concept 'cat' these colored shapes are comprehended as a cat. There are obviously innumerable empirical concepts at our disposal for speaking about what we intuit. What concerns us here, however, is not empirical concepts but rather those concepts that are a priori.

If the understanding is the faculty of making judgments by means of concepts, then it seems clear that we can discover the fundamental concepts of the understanding, which Kant calls categories, by an examination of the form of the judgments themselves. To make a judgment is an activity of the understanding employing concepts, and the logical structure or form of the judgment must therefore be an expression of that category, or those categories, which are used. Kant believes, moreover, that with respect to their logical structure four different forms of judgment are possible, and that in each form there is the possibility of three different kinds of judgments. Let us see how Kant develops this.

First there is a judgment's *quantity*. Every judgment must necessarily have a quantity. If for example the judgment is about cats, it must necessarily say something about all cats, about some cats, or merely about this particular cat. With respect to its quantity, therefore, a judgment is either a universal judgment, a particular judgment or a singular judgment.

A judgment must necessarily also have a *quality*. It must be either affirmative, negative, or what Kant calls 'infinite.' If I say, "This is a cat," I am making an affirmative judgment; if I say, "This is not a cat," that is a negative judgment; if, finally, I say, "This is a not-cat," I have made an infinite judgment. Kant's reason for calling this last kind of judgment infinite is this: In making the judgment that the animal in question is a not-cat, I have therewith placed that creature in the infinite domain (or unlimited class) of that which is not included under the concept 'cat.' Although the infinite judgment is an affirmative judgment, it is still different from the proper affirmative judgment, "This is a cat." For there I have placed the animal about which I am making the judgment in the limited domain (or the limited class) of all that is included under the concept 'cat.'

A judgment must further have a *relation*. Kant distinguishes between three kinds of relations: categorical, hypothetical, and disjunctive judgments. Kant has in mind here that in the categorical judgment there is a relation between subject and predicate. If I say, "This cat is gray," the essential thing about this judgment is that it ascribes the predicate 'gray' to the cat that is referred to in the subject as 'this cat.' The logical structure of the judgment is a subject-predicate relation. In the hypothetical judgment there is a relation between ground and consequence. In the judgment "If there is lightning, then there will be thunder," what is stated is that in case there is lightning, the lightning will be the reason for the subsequent thunder, i.e., the thunder will be the consequence of the fact that there is lightning. Finally, a disjunctive judgment states that two or more judgments exclude each other, that one and only one of them is true, and that all the judgments that comprise the disjunction exhaust all possibilities. If I say, "He is either a carpenter or a mason or a police officer," I have (according to Kant's use of disjunction) asserted that the relation is such that if, for example, he is a carpenter, then what is thereby said is that he is neither a mason nor a police officer. In saying that he is either a carpenter or a mason or a police officer I am therewith excluding all other possibilities. He cannot, for example, be a farmer. In other words, what is affirmed is that he is one of the three mentioned things. If I know that he is neither a mason nor a police officer, then I thereby also know that he is a carpenter.

Finally, every judgment has a *modality*; it is either possibly true, or it is true as a matter of fact, or it is necessarily true. That I shall live to be over eighty years of age cannot be excluded beforehand, but neither can it be maintained as certain. It is possible, neither more nor less. Kant calls such judgments 'problematic,' by which he does not mean the same thing as 'doubtful,' but only that the truth value of the judgment in question is possibly true, possibly not. That Kant was born in 1724 and died in 1804 is a fact. It is not merely something possible, and hence this is not a problematic judgment. The judgment can be put forth as factually true. Such judgments Kant calls 'assertoric.' Since I do not have knowledge either of the factors that caused his birth to take place on the twenty-second of April and not, for example, on the twenty-third of April, or of the factors that resulted in his death on the twelfth of February rather than on the thirteenth of February, I cannot say that the judgment is necessarily true. If I had such knowledge, I would, according to Kant, be entitled to call it a necessarily true judgment. Such judgments Kant calls 'apodictic.' We thus get the following arrangement of the different judgments (Kant's table of judgments is found in B 95):

1.
Quantity
Universal
Particular
Singular

2.
Quality
Affirmative
Negative
Infinite

3.
Relation
Categorical
Hypothetical
Disjunctive

4.
Modality
Problematic
Assertoric
Apodictic

Kant has often been criticized for having accepted this classification of the judgments of logic as complete. He took logic as he found it in his time and somewhat dogmatically supposed that it was eternal and unchanging truth.[1] That this, however, was not the case the intervening years have shown. In the first place, not all judgments can be classified as subject-predicate judgments. Existential judgments, for example, cannot be viewed

[1] In B VIII Kant says: "That logic has already, from the earliest times, proceeded upon this sure path is evidenced by the fact that since Aristotle it was not required to retrace a single step, unless, indeed, we care to count as improvements the removal of certain needless subtleties or the clearer exposition of its recognised teaching, features which concern the elegance rather than the certainty of the science. It is remarkable also that to the present day this logic has not been able to advance a single step, and is thus to all appearance a closed and completed body of doctrine."

as subject-predicate judgments.[2] The judgment, "The author of *Waverley* exists," is not a judgment of this sort, and one seeks in vain in Kant's table under 'relation' to find a place for it. In the second place, with respect to numbers, the nature of truth functions, logical constants, and quantifiers,[3] logic has become far more sophisticated, and the absolute character of Kant's division and arrangement is thereby seriously shaken. It also seems somewhat arbitrary that under 'relation' there are found, in addition to the categorical judgment, only the hypothetical and the disjunctive judgments. Why not, for example, the conjunctive judgment? The answer to this is presumably, at least partially, Kant's desire to have three and only three kinds of judgments under each of the four forms, for only if there were three judgments, could his system of categories work out neatly.

It ought to be emphasized that Kant does not use his account and classification of judgments as a *proof* of what categories there are. What he wishes to do in this section, which he calls "The Clue to the Discovery of All Pure Concepts of the Understanding" (*Von dem Leitfaden der Entdeckung allerreinen Verstandesbegriffe*), is to show by means of the nature of judgments which categories we in fact use. The proof that the categories found here really are categories, that is, that they are necessary conditions of knowledge, Kant gives (or thinks he has given) in his famous section about the deduction of the

[2] Cf. among others Bertrand Russell, "The Philosophy of Logical Atomism," Lecture 6. Cf. also Bertrand Russell, "On Denoting," in *Mind* (1905), reprinted in *Logic and Knowledge: Essays 1901–1950*, ed. Robert Charles Marsh (London: Allen & Unwin, 1956; New York: Macmillan), pp. 41–56.

[3] The judgments, "The author of *Waverley* is dead" and "Scott is dead," are logically speaking two different judgments. (Thus the former uses the so-called iota-operator; the latter does not.) But according to Kant both must be classified as singular judgments.

categories (*Der Deduktion der reinen Verstandesbegriffe*). The criticism that can be leveled at Kant's view of the logical nature of judgment does not therefore strike at the heart of his doctrine of the categories. The way of discovery and the way of proof are, as is well known, not identical; history offers abundant evidence that many a fruitful idea or hypothesis—an idea or hypothesis that has finally yielded to proof or verification—has arisen out of incorrect arguments.

But what categories, what pure (i.e., a priori) concepts of the understanding, does Kant think can be derived from the different kinds of judgment?

Let us first look at judgments with respect to their quantity. As we saw above, we have the following three kinds of judgments:

Universal
Particular
Singular

If I make the judgment that all cats are gray or, in general terms, that all *S* is *P*, I have created a unity, a unity that does not exist as a matter of course, does not exist of itself, does not exist empirically, but has been brought about by an act of the understanding, i.e., by the use of a concept. I have conceptually grasped all *S* (whatever *S* may stand for) as a unity. This I can do, Kant believes, only by using the category (the pure concept of the understanding) *unity*. Without this category it would not be possible to make a judgment about all of the infinitely many existing *S*'s treated as a single concept, a single class, namely the class of all *S*.

In the particular judgment, "Some *S* is *P*," no unity is formed out of what is given. It is not a matter of putting all the *S*'s together in a class and creating a unity, nor is the judgment concerned simply with a single S. The judgment is about *some* S's. The concept that is needed in order to distinguish between all S's and a single S is, according to Kant, the concept *plurality*.

Finally there are singular judgments. I can express this kind of judgment either by using the form, "This S is P," or by giving a name to this S, for example 'John,' thereby getting the judgment, "John is P." What I make the judgment about is not simply a part of this S or of John, but is the whole considered as a unity; it is about *all* that pertains to this S or to John. The category is, therefore, according to Kant, *totality*. The categories that correspond to the three forms of judgment under 'quantity' are these:

Judgments	*Categories*
Universal (*allgemeine*)	Unity (*Einheit*)
Particular (*besondere*)	Plurality (*Vielheit*)
Singular (*einzelne*)	Totality (*Allheit*)

Kant maintains that the third category (totality) is a combination of the first (unity) and the second (plurality). If one applies the category 'unity' to the category 'plurality,' the result is 'totality.' And this, Kant thinks, is not only the case with these three categories, but is also the case with the remaining three times three categories, corresponding to the three remaining forms of judgment.[4]

Let us next look at judgments with respect to their quality. We have the following three kinds of judgments:

[4] On Kant's observation: "Further, it may be observed that the third category in each class always arises from the combination of the second category with the first" (B 110), Richard Falckenberg makes the following comment: "It is this 'neat' remark by Kant which has occasioned Fichte's Triaden and Hegel's dialectical method (*Hilfsbuch zur Geschichte der Philosophie seit Kant*, p. 13).

Affirmative
Negative
Infinite

In an affirmative judgment we assert that something *is* something or other; for example, that *S* is *P*. In other words we affirm that this *S* with its property *P* is a reality. In a negative judgment it is maintained, on the other hand, that something *is not* something or other, for example, that *S* is not *P*. In other words, what is denied is that this *S* with its property *P* is a reality. The categories corresponding to affirmative and negative judgments are therefore respectively *reality* and *negation*. In an infinite judgment, i.e., a judgment of the form, "*S* is not-*P*," it is asserted that *S* has an infinite domain (namely everything that is not-*P*) but yet also that *P* limits this infinite domain. The category is therefore *limitation*. Here, too, we note that if we combine 'reality' and 'negation,' we get 'limitation.'

The categories that correspond to the three forms of judgment under 'quality' are then these:

Judgments	*Categories*
Affirmative (*bejahende*)	Reality (*Realität*)
Negative (*verneinende*)	Negation (*Verneinung*)
Infinite (*unendliche*)	Limitation (*Begrenzung*)

Under relation we have the following three kinds of judgments:

Categorical
Hypothetical
Disjunctive

By a categorical judgment Kant means a judgment of the form, "*S* is *P*." As an example let us take the judgment, "This table is yellow." Here a distinction is made between the thing (the substance) and one of its properties, namely the property 'yellow.' While this property, this yellow color, exists as a sense impression, the thing itself does not exist—in any case in a certain understanding of the word 'exist'—as a sense observation. For whatever is set down as a sense observation will always be conceived of not as the thing, but as one of its properties. That we cannot identify the thing with its properties in the way Hume tried to, is already apparent in the fact that the concept 'property,' in order not to lose all meaning, must be a property of something. And that we cannot do without the concept 'property' stems, Kant believes, from the categorical subject-predicate judgment. For in this judgment we attribute to a subject (a substance) a property; we ascribe a predicate to the subject. Just as the concepts 'thing' and 'property' are necessary tools for the understanding of what is given to us in sensation, so the categorical judgment is necessary to the form of thought. The category that is reflected in the categorical judgment Kant calls *Inhärenz und subsistenz* (*substantia et accidens*). Let us here simply call this category *substance*. It is a pure concept of the understanding, hence a category, for we have not formed the concept 'substance' by abstraction; on the contrary, it is by means of the concept 'substance' that we understand the empirically given as things and as properties of things.

A hypothetical judgment is a judgment of the form "If *p* then *q*," where *p* and *q* are two judgments of whatever kind. Consider the example, "If it is raining, then the street is wet." [5]

[5] Kant's own rather more exalted example reads: "If there is a perfect justice, the obstinately wicked are punished" (B 98). The example has, however, the shortcoming that it is virtually (not to say entirely) a tautology.

This judgment does not imply that either of the two included judgments (namely the judgments [1] it is raining and [2] the street is wet) is true; what is being said is, rather, that the truth of the one judgment must be considered as the basis for the truth of the other. The hypothetical judgment cannot be made (its thought cannot be expressed) except by means of the concept *causality* (or *dependence*). Without this concept we would never be able to think, to comprehend, or to understand anything other than temporal succession. As Hume also showed, we cannot learn anything about causality by confining ourselves to what is given in sensation; on the contrary, it is causality as a pure concept of the understanding that enables us to comprehend what is given empirically as causally connected.

The disjunctive judgment says that either the statement p is true or the statement q is true. It is generally recognized that such a judgment can be understood in two ways. It can be understood in the sense that we are saying either p is true or q is true, i.e., perhaps they are both true ("On his bookshelves you will only find books by Kant or by Hume"); or it can be understood to mean that we are saying that either p is true or q is true, but that they are not both true ("The meetings are led either by the chairman or by the vice-chairman"). It is in this last sense (the so-called exclusive meaning) that Kant here takes the disjunctive judgment. In other words, if p is true (the meetings are led by the chairman) then it has to follow that q is false (the meetings are not let by the vice-chairman). And if q is true (the meetings are led by the vice-chairman) then it has to follow that p is false (the meetings are not led by the chairman). The contrary, consequently, also holds: if p is false, then q is true; and if q is false, then p is true. P and q are dependent on each other; they affect each other mutually. The disjunctive judgment expresses therefore the category that Kant calls *community* (*der Gemeinschaft*).[6]

As is the case with the third category under both 'quantity' and 'quality,' 'community' can be seen as conditioned by (but not derived from) the two preceding categories. The categories that are brought into play by the category 'community,' understood as an interaction between things (substances), are 'substance' and 'causality.'

The judgments and categories under 'relation' are, then, these:

Judgments	*Categories*	(*Inhärenz und Subsistenz*)
Categorical	Substance	(*substantia et accidens*)
Hypothetical	Causality	(*Kausalität und Dependenz*)
Disjunctive	Community	(*Ursache und Wirkung*)
		(*Gemeinschaft*)
		(*Wechselwirkung zwischen dem Handelnden und Leidenden*)

Finally there are the judgments under 'modality.' The making of problematic judgments depends upon the existence of the category *possibility*. In the case of assertoric judgments it is maintained that something not only is possible but that it is also actually the case. The category that is emphasized in an assertoric judgment is *existence* (*dasein*). It is by means of this category that we can assert that something not only is a possibility but that it also exists. Finally, without the category *necessity* we could not make apodictic judgments; for in an

[6] "Finally, the disjunctive judgment contains a relation of two or more propositions to each other, a relation not, however, of a logical sequence, but of logical opposition in so far as the sphere of the one excludes the sphere of the other, and yet at the same time of community, in so far as the propositions taken together occupy the whole sphere of the knowledge in question" (B 99).

apodictic judgment we maintain not only that something or other actually is the case; we affirm, as well, that it is so by necessity.

The possible is that which is in accordance with the conditions of intuition and thought.[7] To be free of contradiction is thus a necessary but not a sufficient condition. For example, it is not self-contradictory, according to Kant, to speak of a figure included by two straight lines. Such a figure is nonetheless an impossibility. It does not satisfy the a priori conditions that are determined by space as an a priori form of intuition. That something is the case, that something that is possible also exists, means either that it is the object of immediate sense observation or that it is connected with (can be viewed as the effect of) something else that can be the object of immediate sense observation.[8]

The third category, 'necessity,' in which the two previous categories (the categories 'possibility' and 'existence') are included, is thus that which not only is possible and not only can be connected with something that can be the object of immediate sense observation, but in addition is determined to be the effect of given causes.[9] Since nothing happens except what is determined by law, so nothing occurs unless the category 'necessity' is employed; or rather, unless it could be employed if one had the requisite knowledge.[10]

[7] "That which agrees with the formal conditions of experience, that is, with the conditions of intuition and of concepts, is *possible*" (B 265).

[8] "That which is bound up with the material conditions of experience, that is, with sensation, is *actual*" (B 266).

[9] "That which in its connection with the actual is determined in accordance with universal conditions of experience, is (that is, exists as) *necessary*" (B 266).

[10] "That everything which happens is hypothetically necessary is a principle which subordinates alteration in the world to a law, that is, to a rule of necessary existence, without which there would be nothing that could be entitled nature" (B 280).

Under modality the judgments and categories are then the following:

Judgments	*Categories*
Problematic	Possibility–impossibility
Assertoric	Existence–not-existence (*dasein-Nichtsein*)
Apodictic	Necessity–contingency

The assembled table of categories looks like this:

Quantity
unity
plurality
totality

Quality
reality
negation
limitation

Relation
substance
causality
community

Modality
possibility–impossibility
existence–nonexistence
necessity–contingency

The categories under 'quantity' and 'quality' Kant calls 'the mathematical categories'; these categories indicate the conditions for making judgments about objects in space and time. The categories under 'relation' and 'modality' Kant calls 'the dynamic categories'; these indicate how an object is determined in relation to other objects.

It ought again to be emphasized that Kant, by examining the possible and necessary forms of judgments, thinks he has discovered all the categories, but he does not think he has demonstrated their validity. It is one thing to have shown that we actually do use categories; it is quite another to have proved that our employment of categories is legitimate. It is this latter point that Kant attempts to prove in the section dealing with the transcendental deduction of the concepts of the understanding (*Von der Deduktion der reinen Verstandesbegriffe*). What he there tries to prove is that we are right in using categories; he does not prove that we are right in using just those categories which we actually do employ. This he proves in the section "The Analytic of Principles" (*Die Analytik der Grundsätze*). He attempts to prove the mathematical categories in the sections he calls "Axioms of Intuition" and "Anticipations of Perception," while he attempts to establish the dynamic categories in the sections he calls "Analogies of Experience" and "The Postulates of Empirical Thought." Corresponding to the table of categories we thus get the following table or schema of the principles:

Axioms of Intuition
Anticipations of Perception   Analogies of Experience
The Postulates of Empirical Thought

THE TRANSCENDENTAL DEDUCTION

Kant believes he has shown that there are twelve and only twelve categories, i.e., twelve and only twelve pure concepts of the understanding. What he thinks he has shown, so far, is only what, in fact, is the case, a *quid facti*, as Kant also expresses it. The categories that do in fact exist he thinks he has established in the section, "The Clue to the Discovery of all Pure Concepts of the Understanding" (*Von dem Leitfaden der Entdeckung aller reinen Verstandesbegriffe*), a section often referred to as 'the metaphysical deduction.' The transcendental deduction is not, however, a question of *quid facti*, but of *quid juris*. It is not a question about how extensively we actually employ categories, but a question of whether our use of categories is legitimate. In other words, is the use of categories a necessary condition of knowledge? If the answer is affirmative, the use of categories is justified; if it is negative, the use of categories is not justified.

A first point on that difficult road which leads through the transcendental deduction is what Kant calls 'the manifold of representations' (sense impressions). Sense experience is a manifold of various sense impressions. These different sense impressions are, as Hume maintained, unconnected. There is no extra sense impression of something that binds them into a unity. To combine sense impressions into a unity is therefore an act of the understanding, a synthesis.

In the first edition of *The Critique of Pure Reason* Kant gives a psychologically oriented explanation (what he calls the subjective deduction) of the nature of the synthesis. He distinguishes here between *apprehension, reproduction,* and *recognition.*

Every intuition takes place in time, for time is an a priori condition of all intuition.[11] We say that during a given period of time we are able to look at the *same* thing. Anything that is seen through several successive moments is seen as one and the same. Yet in each of these moments we have a sense impression. Let us say that we look at a thing from time t_1 to time t_5. At t_1 we have the sense impression S_1. At t_2 we have

[11] "Our representations, whether they are due to the influence of outer things, or are produced through inner causes, whether they arise *a priori*, or being appearances have an empirical origin, they must all, as modifications of the mind, belong to inner sense. All our knowledge is thus finally subject to time, the formal condition of inner sense. In it they must all be ordered, connected, and brought into relation. This is a general observation which, throughout what follows, must be borne in mind as being quite fundamental" (A 98–99).

the sense impression S_2. At t_3 we have the sense impression S_3; at t_4 we have S_4, and finally at t_5 we have the impression S_5. Now these sense impressions (the sense impressions S_1—S_5) are five different sense impressions—different in the sense in which, for example, five successive blows on the head are different. But we would never say that we had had five successive sense impressions in the period of time t_1 to t_5. What we say is that we have looked at (intuited) one and the same thing during the period of time that has elapsed. In other words, we have created a unity out of that which was not a unity. By an *apprehension*, that which is a manifold is synthesized as a unity.

Such an apprehension is only possible if the different sense impressions are combined or held together. If this were not the case, the conditions for speaking about one and the same object would not be present. Instead, we would only be able to speak about a succession of different sense impressions. But to retain a sense impression that has already vanished is only possible if the imagination *reproduces* it. Not only must the imagination reproduce the earlier sense impression; these sense impressions must also be capable of being cognized, or rather, be capable of being recognized, as just these sense impressions. As Kant puts it, there must be *recognition*.

The synthesis must not be viewed as a process that takes place in three stages—the first phase 'apprehension,' the next 'reproduction,' and the last 'recognition.' These are but three aspects of one and the same process—aspects that must necessarily be present if intuiting an object consists in receiving a succession of sense impressions. That the intuition of an object consists in the receiving of such a succession, and therefore consists in the combining of a manifold, Kant thinks to be necessary, since the intuition necessarily takes place in time.

That the intuition of an object is the intuition of a manifold of combined sense impressions is thus not a matter of experience; it is an a priori assertion.[12] The synthesis is not empirical but a priori. It is a synthesis that expresses the unity of consciousness. 'Apprehension,' 'reproduction,' and 'recognition'—the three aspects of the synthesis—are necessary conditions for knowing an object. They are concepts that presuppose a consciousness. The consciousness must be a unity; it must be one and the same consciousness, for recognition is precisely what constitutes the unity of consciousness.

Let us suppose that there were no such thing as recognition. Every sense impression lasted only an instant. Immediately afterwards it was gone, to be followed at once by another sense impression just as short-lived. When each sense impression was gone, consciousness could remember nothing about it. And even if a sense impression could be reproduced, it would not be perceived as a reproduced sense impression, i.e., as one that had occurred earlier, but rather as a sense impression that had never before existed. In such a situation the necessary and sufficient conditions for employing the concept 'the same consciousness' would not be present, because the concept 'same' can, in this context, only be the concept 'the same as before.' Nor would the conditions for using the concept 'consciousness' be present. Where it is logically impossible to speak of a consciousness as being the *same* consciousness, one cannot speak

[12] "In order that unity of intuition may arise out of this manifold (as is required in the representation of space) it must first be run through, and held together. This act I name the *synthesis of apprehension*, because it is directed immediately upon intuition, which does indeed offer a manifold, but a manifold which can never be represented as a manifold, and as contained *in a single representation*, save in virtue of such a synthesis.

"This synthesis of apprehension must also be exercised *a priori*, that is, in respect of representations which are not empirical. For without it we should never have *a priori* the representations either of space or of time" (A 99).

of consciousness at all; and since the application of a concept requires that successive sense impressions be recognized as belonging under this concept, the use of concepts would thus be out of the question. But if it is impossible to use any concepts, then it is impossible to have any knowledge of objects.[13]

What we have seen thus far is this: To intuit is to intuit in time (for time is an a priori form of intuition). This entails intuition as a synthesis of a manifold—a synthesis constituted by apprehension, reproduction, and recognition. Without such a synthesis there is no self-consciousness (or even consciousness), and without such a synthesis there is no object—no object, that is, as a synthesis of a manifold of various sense impressions in time.

These three concepts, the synthesis, knowledge of an object, and the unity of consciousness (self-consciousness), are, in other words, logically interdependent. Without the synthesis there is no possibility of the other two. And if you have one of the two others, then you necessarily have the remaining two also.

To comprehend intuitions as objects is, however, a necessary condition for speaking of knowledge at all. The object as a synthesis of a manifold is a necessity if there is to be any knowledge whatsoever.

We now find ourselves at an important point in the Transcendental Deduction (in the first edition's version). We are at

[13] "The word 'concept' might of itself suggest this remark. For this unitary consciousness is what combines the manifold, successively intuited, and thereupon also reproduced, into one representation. This consciousness may often be only faint, so that we do not connect it with the act itself, that is, not in any direct manner with the *generation* of the representation, but only with the outcome (that which is thereby represented). But notwithstanding these variations, such consciousness, however indistinct, must always be present; without it, concepts, and therewith knowledge of objects, are altogether impossible" (A 103–104).

the transition from the subjective deduction to the objective deduction.

What are we to understand by an object? Suppose I see something. The question (my own or another's) as to what it is I am seeing must necessarily be answered so that the answer involves a judgment—a judgment as to *what* it is that is seen. It is this *what* that is the object of knowledge. It is the subject in the judgment that answers the question as to what it is I see. Obviously this does not have to be an object in the sense of a material object (unless we want to claim that only material objects can be seen); seeing a triangle or an exercise in arithmetic written on the blackboard is also a matter of seeing an object. It is an object in the sense that it is the subject of the judgment that constitutes an answer to the question as to what it is that is seen and of which different things can be predicated. To be an object is, in other words, to be something that is conceptually determined; it is something that is understood by means of a concept. The concept 'object' (in this sense of the concept) is thus necessary for knowledge. As Kant puts it, it is a necessary condition of order and coherence in knowledge.[14]

If I say that I see an orange, the object is not identical with any particular sense experience of it. To call what I see an 'orange' is to apply the concept 'orange' to it. It is to bring everything that is seen, felt, smelled, and tasted under that concept. It is to order under a rule what is seen, felt, tasted,

[14] This important passage runs as follows: "Now we find that our thought of the relation of all knowledge to its object carries with it an element of necessity; the object is viewed as that which prevents our modes of knowledge from being haphazard or arbitrary, and which determines them *a priori* in some definite fashion. For in so far as they are to relate to an object, they must necessarily agree with one another, that is, must possess that unity which constitutes the concept of an object" (A 104).

and smelled. The concept 'object' is what makes it possible to understand what is seen;[15] it enables us to make statements. In general it is a condition for being able to use a language about what is given to the senses. Without the concept 'object' there would be no experience. This concept is therefore not the sort that is formed through experience—for example by abstraction —for it is a condition of experience. The concept 'object' reflects the unity of consciousness. And this unity, as we have seen, is not empirically ascertained but is established a priori. The unity of consciousness is consequently a transcendental condition. This condition Kant calls the *transcendental apperception.*[16]

In the second edition's version of the transcendental deduction little is said about the synthesis of the manifold. It is considered almost as an established fact that such a synthesis exists, not as something given in sensation, but as the result of the activity of the understanding—i.e., as the result of the use of concepts. From this fact (or rather, from what he considers as a fact) Kant arrives at the transcendental apperception

[15] "At this point we must make clear to ourselves what we mean by the expression 'an object of representations.' We have stated above that appearances are themselves nothing but sensible representations, which, as such and in themselves, must not be taken as objects capable of existing outside our power of representation. What, then, is to be understood when we speak of an object corresponding to, and consequently also distinct from, our knowledge? It is easily seen that this object must be thought only as something in general $= x$, since outside our knowledge we have nothing which we could set over against this knowledge as corresponding to it" (A 104).

[16] "All necessity, without exception, is grounded in a transcendental condition. There must, therefore, be a transcendental ground of the unity of consciousness in the synthesis of the manifold of all our intuitions, and consequently also of the concepts of objects in general, and so of all objects of experience, a ground without which it would be impossible to think any object for our intuitions; for this object is no more than that something, the concept of which expresses such a necessity of synthesis.

"This original and transcendental condition is no other than *transcendental apperception*" (A 106).

in the following way. The concept 'combination' presupposes the concept 'manifold.' If there were no manifold out of which to create a synthesis, the concepts 'synthesis' and 'combination' would have no meaning. But the concept 'combination' is only meaningful on the assumption that the concept 'unity' already exists. To combine is necessarily to combine something into a unity that is not already a unity (the concept 'to seek' presupposes the concept 'to find,' the concept 'to attempt' presupposes the concept 'to succeed,' and the concept 'to clothe' presupposes the concept 'to be clothed'). The concept 'unity' is consequently not an empirical concept. We do not begin with the concept 'to combine' in order then, by observation of the results, to create the concept 'unity.' We simply cannot speak about combination without presupposing the concept 'unity.' The concept 'unity' is consequently a priori and is a logical presupposition of the remaining concepts. It is therefore also a logical presupposition of the categories (and thus also of the category 'unity').

But Kant speaks not only of the *concept* of unity. He speaks also of the unity of *consciousness*. The argument (the second edition's version) is this: Every thought, every representation, must necessarily be a thought or a representation that belongs to someone. There must necessarily always be a person who can say that this thought or this representation is his.

Of every thought, every judgment, every statement (including also statements about what is given in intuition) it is a logical necessity that we be able to ask whose thought it is, who passed the judgment, who made the statement. And it is a logical necessity that there is a person who can answer, "I thought it," "I passed it," "I stated it." Whatever a person thinks or intuits must necessarily always be *his* thought or his intuition, and this holds true universally. An 'I think' must accompany every person's thought, intuition, or representation. It is, however, important to note that this 'I' we are speaking of here is not identical with any empirical contents of consciousness. This 'I think' is not identical with empirical self-consciousness. For of all empirical thought-content (and so also of empirical self-consciousness) we must necessarily be able to say that it is *mine*. This 'I' is therefore a transcendental 'I.' And this transcendental 'I' that possesses the contents of consciousness that I have at the moment, is identical with the transcendental 'I' that possessed the contents of my consciousness yesterday. This transcendental 'I' is a necessary condition of every thought, every judgment, every assertion, every idea—and thus also of consciousness itself. This 'I' is what Kant (as in the first edition's version) calls 'transcendental apperception' or 'original apperception' or 'pure apperception.' It is this transcendental apperception that is the fundamental condition of all knowledge.[17]

Transcendental apperception—the transcendental 'I'—is not itself an act of consciousness. If it were, I would have to say

[17] "It must be possible for the 'I think' to accompany all my representations; for otherwise something would be represented in me which could not be thought at all, and that is equivalent to saying that the representation would be impossible, or at least would be nothing to me. That representation which can be given prior to all thought is entitled intuition. All the manifold of intuition has, therefore, a necessary relation to the 'I think' in the same subject in which this manifold is found. But this representation is an act of *spontaneity*, that is, it cannot be regarded as belonging to sensibility. I call it *pure apperception*, to distinguish it from empirical apperception, or, again, *original apperception*, because it is that self-consciousness which, while generating the representation 'I think' (a representation which must be capable of accompanying all other representations, and which in all consciousness is one and the same), cannot itself be accompanied by any further representation. The unity of this apperception I likewise entitle the *transcendental* unity of self-consciousness, in order to indicate the possibility of *a priori* knowledge arising from it" (B 132).

again of this act of consciousness that it is *mine* (would have to assert an 'I think')—or rather, if it were an act of consciousness, then it could be structured conceptually and thereby could be made into an object for a judgment—not only a judgment that thus would have a subject (namely that which the judgment is about) but also a judgment that presupposed an 'I' that set forth the judgment. The final logical presupposition of an act of consciousness cannot itself be an act of consciousness. It was therefore a logical misunderstanding when Hume thought he could show that no 'I' exists by showing that there was no sense impression of such an 'I.' For had there been such a sense impression, then it would have presupposed another 'I' that had this sense impression. All that can be said about this 'I' (and therefore also about transcendental apperception) is simply that it is an expression of the necessary unity of consciousness, a unity that manifests itself in the fact that all that is said, thought, and represented must necessarily always be able to be combined with an 'I.' To speak about pure apperception or the pure 'I' is not to speak of an act, a process, or a thing, but about the fundamental logical condition of having concepts like 'judgment,' 'assertion,' and 'consciousness.'

The connection between pure apperception and the categories Kant establishes through an examination of judgments. Compare the following two judgments: (1) "Bodies have weight"; and (2) "When I lift this body, I note a pressure on the hand that lifts it." One difference between (1) and (2) is that (1) expresses objective knowledge about bodies, while (2) does not. In (2) no objective connection is made between the concepts 'body' and 'weight.' Such an objective connection is, however, found in (1); there we have a unity, a synthesis, of these two concepts. The concept 'body' and the concept 'weight' are, so to say, thought together in the object (i.e., in the judgment's subject). Judgment (2) is subjective; it reports only what I notice when I lift the body and implies nothing about what others will notice. It says nothing at all about the concepts 'body' and 'weight' being in some way connected. Judgment (1), on the other hand, is objective. It implies that regardless of who lifts a body, that person will notice a pressure. The concepts 'body' and 'weight' are brought into an objective unity in the sense that this declared unity is independent of what is subjective, but also in the sense that the two concepts are united in an object.[18]

But this objective unity is an expression of and is determined by pure apperception and does not exist independently of it.

We can summarize as follows: Knowledge is to be found only in objective judgments. Only in such judgments is the intuited comprehended and understood; only in them can it be thought and therefore known (intuition without concepts is blind). Objective judgments (and thereby knowledge) are dependent upon pure apperception. Kant thinks that in the metaphysical deduction he has established all forms of judgments and thereby found those concepts that find expression in and make possible these judgments. Thus we see that these judgments (and judgments other than these that were established in the metaphysical deduction do not, according to Kant, exist) are necessary conditions of knowledge; and if these judgments

[18] "But if I investigate more precisely the relation of the given modes of knowledge in any judgment, and distinguish it, as belonging to the understanding, from the relation according to laws of the reproductive imagination, which has only subjective validity, I find that judgment is nothing but the manner in which given modes of knowledge are brought to the objective unity of apperception. This is what is intended by the copula 'is.' It is employed to distinguish the objective unity of given representations from the subjective. It indicates their relation to original apperception, and its *necessary unity*. It holds good even if the judgment is itself empirical, and therefore contingent, as, for example, in the judgment, 'Bodies are heavy' " (B 142).

are necessary conditions of knowledge, then the concepts (categories) that find expression in and condition these judgments must also be necessary conditions of knowledge.

Let us sum up the transcendental deduction by means of the following seven points:

I. There exists a synthesis of a manifold. The existence of this synthesis is not discovered empirically, but is an a priori truth.

II. The synthesis (an apprehension by means of reproduction and recognition) is an expression of the unity of consciousness.

III. The object (the synthesis of the manifold) and the unity of consciousness thus determine each other.

IV. The unity of consciousness (and thereby also the unity of the object) is a necessary condition of experience. It is this unity that makes it possible (is an a priori condition) that the 'I' that is now thinking is the same 'I' that was thinking before and will be thinking a little while from now.

V. As an a priori and necessary condition of experience this unity is called pure or transcendental apperception.

VI. This is to say that pure apperception is a necessary condition of (1) the synthesis of the manifold, (2) the unity of the object, (3) the use of concepts, and (4) passing judgments. (1), (2), (3), and (4) are, however, different expressions for one and the same thing.

VII. To make judgments is only possible by means of concepts. The categories (cf. the metaphysical deduction) are therefore necessary conditions of knowledge.

From the foregoing it appears that knowledge requires two things: on the one hand intuition (that which is given in space and time), and on the other the application of categories to what is given in intuition. Neither intuition alone nor categories alone can give knowledge. Categories without intuition are empty, and intuition without categories is blind. The categories are therefore necessary conditions of empirical knowledge. Such empirical knowledge is what Kant calls experience.[19]

The categories are necessary conditions of experience. Everything that is conceived and comprehended is conceived and comprehended consequently by means of the categories. The reason why nature follows a priori laws is because it can be conceived only by means of the categories. Of course the categories prescribe only a priori laws, laws that hold for nature as such (*die Natur überhaupt*). The particular, empirical laws of nature cannot be prescribed by the categories nor can they be derived from them; they must be determined empirically. But even though they cannot be derived from the categories, they must necessarily be in agreement with them.[20]

[19] "Even, therefore, with the aid of (pure) intuition, the categories do not afford us any knowledge of things; they do so only through their possible application to *empirical intuition*. In other words, they serve only for the possibility of *empirical knowledge;* and such knowledge is what we entitle experience. Our conclusion is therefore this: the categories, as yielding knowledge of *things,* have no kind of application, save only in regard to things which may be objects of possible experience" (B 147–48).

[20] "Pure understanding is not, however, in a position, through mere categories, to prescribe to appearances any *a priori* laws other than those which are involved in a *nature in general,* that is, in the conformity to the law of all appearances in space and time. Special laws, as concerning those appearances which are empirically determined, cannot in their specific character be *derived* from the categories, although they are one and all subject to them. To obtain any knowledge whatsoever of these special laws, we must resort to experience; but it is the *a priori* laws that alone can instruct us in regard to experience in general, and as to what it is that can be known as an object of experience" (B 165).

THE SCHEMATISM

It is by means of categories that we comprehend and understand what is given in space and time.[21] That something is comprehended by means of a category signifies, according to Kant, that it is subsumed under the category in question. The concept 'cat' is an empirical concept, and to use this concept means that something that is intuited is subsumed under it. If I point to an animal and say: "This is a cat," then I have used the concept 'cat.' A condition of using a concept is, according to Kant, that there is a likeness between the concept and that to which the concept is applied. And this is the case, Kant asserts, with an empirical concept and that to which this concept is properly applicable. Admittedly, the concept 'cat' has neither four legs nor whiskers, but in accordance with its definition the concept determines that those animals which can correctly be called cats must have (among other things) four legs and whiskers. The definition of the concept contains empirical determinants. There are therefore no fundamental problems attached to the use of empirical concepts.

It is otherwise with the pure concepts of the understanding, i.e., with the categories. Here it is not a question of the likeness between the concept and that to which the concept is applied. The concepts are pure, i.e., without empirical content, and therefore cannot bear a likeness to anything empirical. The categories cannot be read out of experience, for they are the

[21] It is worth remembering that we are not here speaking about two mental processes, which take place so to say in two stages: first an intuition in space and time and afterwards the comprehending of what is intuited. To have intuited something is also to have comprehended it by means of categories. Or expressed otherwise, to intuit entails judgment about what is intuited, that already involves the use of categories.

prescribers of it. No one will maintain, says Kant, that the category 'causality' exists as something that is given in sense. There is a chasm between a category and that to which the category is applied.

In order to throw a bridge over this chasm, there is required, as Kant puts it, some third thing, something that has likeness both to the pure concept and to what is given in sensation, something that at one and the same time is both intellectual and sensory. Kant calls this third element the transcendental schema and concludes that the schema must be time. For time as the a priori form of intuition satisfies both requirements. It is a priori, but it is at the same time a condition for all intuition, inner as well as outer. Intuition is possible only if it takes place in time. Time is thus the element that makes possible the application of the categories to what is intuited. Before a category can be used it must therefore be combined with time. By being subject to the transcendental determination of time, a category becomes a schema and as such can be applied to that which exists in intuition.

It is important to distinguish between a concept and a mental image, and between a schema and a mental image. Let us begin with an empirical concept. The concept 'cat' is, of course, not identical with any mental image of a cat. The concept 'cat' cannot be two different things; but a mental image of a cat can be many different things. I can imagine both gray and black cats, both large and small cats, and if cats can be pretty or ugly, both pretty and ugly cats. But to know or to understand the concept 'cat' means at least to be able to imagine a cat and to decide whether some particular animal is a cat. It is to have rules for forming, among other things, mental images of cats. A mental image of a particular animal comes under the concept 'cat' if it is formed by means of this concept's schema.[22]

So far as empirical concepts are concerned, there is no real difference between concept and schema—if, all things considered, there is any difference at all.[23]

Let us look next at the categories. As we have seen, the categories have no likeness to what is given in sensation. They are pure a priori concepts and have consequently nothing empirical in them. The difference between a category and an empirical concept can also be expressed in this way: the empirical concept can be considered as a rule for knowing, recognizing, and imagining the kind of things or the kind of objects of which it is the concept. A category has, on the other hand, no such function. The category 'substance' does not enable us to imagine anything as mysterious as a substance. The category is a universal rule, which is presupposed in the employment of empirical concepts.[24]

[22] "This representation of a universal procedure of imagination in providing an image for a concept, I entitle the schema of this concept" (B 180).

[23] Kant confesses that there is no real difference when he says, "Still less is an object of experience or its image ever adequate to the empirical concept; for this latter always stands in immediate relation to the schema of imagination, as a rule for the determinative of our intuition, in accordance with some specific universal" (B 180). Immediately afterwards, however, Kant seems to identify them: "The concept 'dog' signifies a rule according to which my imagination can delineate the figure of a four-footed animal in a general manner, without limitation to any single determinate figure such as experience, or any possible image that I can represent *in concreto*, actually present" (B 180). At A 106 Kant says that a concept is "something universal which serves as a rule."

[24] "Transcendental philosophy has the peculiarity that besides the rule (or rather the universal condition of rules), which is given in the pure concept of understanding, it can also specify *a priori* the instance to which the rule is to be applied" (B 174). What in this connection is of importance is the remark inside the parentheses: "or rather the universal conditional rules."

Instances of the concept 'cat' are particular cats or mental images of cats. Instances of the category 'substance' are the rules that every empirical concept of any object or other must satisfy. Or to put it another way, the empirical concept is used in assertions about empirical objects, for example, the assertion, "This cat is gray." The category is used in the rules for making empirical assertions. The difference between an empirical concept and a category is thus a difference in logical type: empirical concepts are first-order rules, while the categories, which are rules for rules, are second-order rules.[25]

The connection between the category and what is given in sense is established through the empirical concept, and the connection between the empirical concept and the category is established through the category being a rule for the empirical concept. The category 'substance' is related to the concept 'cat' in the same way that the concept 'cat' is related to a particular cat or to a particular mental image of a cat. But the condition under which a category can give rules for empirical concepts is, according to Kant, that it is schematized, i.e., that it becomes subject to the transcendental determination of time or, if one will, that it gives a priori rules for temporal succession.[26]

From the metaphysical deduction it will be remembered that Kant divides the categories into four groups: quantity, quality, relation, and modality.

Let us first take *quantity*. Kant speaks about the concept 'magnitude.' If the concept 'magnitude' is to be applied to

[25] This is pointed out clearly by Robert Paul Wolff in *Kant's Theory of Mental Activity* (Cambridge, Mass.: Harvard University Press, 1963), p. 212 f.

[26] "The schemata are thus nothing but a priori determinations of time in accordance with rules. These rules relate in the order of the categories to the *time-series*, the *time-content*, the *time-order*, and lastly to the *scope of time* in respect of all possible objects" (B 184).

outer intuition, magnitude must be something that is both spatially extended and exists in time. But not all intuition is outer. Inner intuition is not in space but in time only. The schematized category is therefore the concept of magnitude understood as a magnitude in time. How is a magnitude in time to be understood? It is a magnitude that has become, or becomes, a magnitude by one point in time being added, or having been added, to another. A magnitude in time is something that passes, something that, so to say, moves forward. The *successive* is fundamental for the understanding of time. Moments of time succeed one another. Moments are to be understood as temporal units, and time is to be understood as a succession of these units, which follow one upon the other. Kant arrives, therefore, at number as the schema of quantity (magnitude).[27]

Let us next take *quality*. Under 'quality' we have the categories 'reality,' 'negation,' and 'limitation.' They are the categories that are used when it is maintained that something exists or does not exist. That which exists, that which has reality, must exist in intuition; it must exist as something that can be sensed (as an *Empfindung*). An actual sensation, whether it exists in both space and time or in time only, must have not only a certain magnitude but also a certain intensity. Something can be more or less red, more or less sweet, or more or less sonorous. This red color that I see could have been either stronger or weaker than it actually is. It has a certain fixed degree or intensity, something every sense impression (*Empfindung*) does and must have.

[27] "The pure image of all magnitudes (quantorum) for outer sense is space; that of all objects of the senses in general is time. But the pure schema of magnitude (quantitatis), as a concept of the understanding, is *number*, a representation which comprises the successive of homogeneous units" (B 182).

That which does not exist is necessarily without magnitude, but also necessarily without degree or intensity. There is nothing to be sensible of; there is no *Empfindung*. The transition from reality to negation is thus a transition from a sense impression of minimum intensity to the disappearance of this sense impression. And the transition from negation to reality is a transition from nothing to a sensation of a particular intensity.

Suppose we have a sense impression of a certain degree of intensity. Suppose further that this sense impression subsequently fades away. This change, so far as degrees of intensity are concerned, will necessarily have taken place without any discontinuity. Every existing sensation must be thought of as having arisen by virtue of the fact that all points from zero up to the intensity that it now possesses have been run through. Kant speaks of a synthesis of sense impressions and time.[28] This must not, however, be understood to mean that an existing sensation is created through the execution of such a synthesis (considered as a psychological act) by the one who senses it. What is meant is that the degree of intensity that every sensation necessarily must have can only be understood in terms of its having run, as it were, from nothing through all intermediary degrees up to that degree of intensity that it now has.

Suppose that I touch a radiator and note that it is warm—let us say that it is 95°. A half an hour ago I felt the same radiator and found that it was 68°. I must now necessarily suppose that the radiator in the preceding half hour has run through all the intervening points from 68° to 95°. It would

[28] "We thus find that . . . the schema of quality is the synthesis of sensation or perception with the representation of time; it is the filling of time" (B 184).

be impossible for me to think that it could have skipped over any of the degrees. I simply could not understand how, for example, it could have gone from 72° to 74° without having passed through 73°.

Suppose, however, that I strike a key on the piano. The result is a certain definite tone. It is heard directly with whatever strength it has. I do not hear it coming into being from nothing and continually rising in intensity until it reaches its final strength. Kant admits this.[29] But nonetheless I can only understand the production of the tone by thinking of it as beginning at zero and running continuously through all of the intervening degrees. Kant maintains that it is a synthetic a priori assertion that any sensation that comes into being must begin at zero and develop in unbroken continuity to its particular intensity.

Under *relation,* the schema for the category 'substance' is that which determines our view of what is constant in a process of change. If a piece of wax is warmed, it goes through a series of changes, but it continues to be the same piece of wax. Even if all its properties are changed, the piece of wax, of which these different properties are properties, nonetheless remains one and the same piece of wax. What continues to be the same is not the properties themselves but that of which they are properties, namely the substratum.[30] To say that a change takes place is the same as saying that something changes. To say that this piece of wax changes means that the properties of this piece of wax at a particular time are different from what they were at

[29] "Apprehension by means merely of sensation occupies only an instant, if, that is, I do not take into account the succession of different sensations" (B 209).

[30] "The schema of substance is permanence of the real in time, that is, the representation of the real as a substrate of empirical determination of time in general, and so as abiding while all else changes" (B 183).

some other time. If there were not something that remained unchanged throughout the time during which the change took place, we would be speaking of two different pieces of wax and not of one.

The schema of the category of 'causality' is a succession of events such that when a certain event occurs, it is followed by a second event, determined according to a rule.[31]

As the last category under 'relation' we have the category 'community.' If we have the disjunctive judgment that either *A* has the property *B* or *C* has the property *D*, then this judgment affirms that whether *A* has the property *B* depends upon whether or not *C* has the property *D*. If *C* is *D*, then *A* is not *B*, but if *C* is not *D*, then *A* is *B*. The judgment affirms also that whether or not *C* has the property *D* depends upon whether or not *A* has the property *B*. A determination of what *A* is depends upon a determination of what *C* is, and a determination of what *C* is depends upon a determination of what *A* is. *A* and *B* are mutually dependent upon one another. If we schematize this category, we arrive at this: changes in *A* have their cause in *C*, and changes in *C* have their cause in *A*. In other words there is interaction between *A* and *C*.[32]

Finally we have the categories under *modality*, namely 'possibility'–'impossibility,' 'existence'–'non-existence,' and 'necessity'–'contingency.'

As schematized, the category 'possibility' is empirical possi-

[31] "The schema of cause, and of the causality of a thing in general, is the real upon which, whenever posited, something else always follows. It consists, therefore, in the succession of the manifold, in so far as that succession is subject to a rule" (B 183).

[32] "The schema of community or reciprocal causality of substance in respect of their accidents, is the coexistence, according to a universal rule" (B 183 f.).

bility, not merely logical possibility. A concept of something or other is logically possible only if it does not contain determinations that contradict each other (the concept of a round square is thus a logical impossibility). The concept of a body that moves from one placc to anothcr without traversing all of the intermediary points is not, according to Kant, a concept that contains any logical contradiction; it is, however, a concept that is an empirical impossibility, for it does not satisfy the conditions of experience (cf. the schematized category of 'quantity'). A concept that contains determinations that contradict each other (e.g., to be both warm and not warm) is nonetheless empirically possible where the determinations do not occur at the same time. The concept of a golden mountain is possible in the sense that it is in accordance with the conditions of experience.

To move from 'possibility' to the schema of 'existence' is to move to that which is found in experience. It is to move from that which is possible to that which is actual. A golden mountain ceases to be merely possible and becomes instead actual only where someone at some point or other in time has established its existence experientially.

The schema of necessity is 'existence,' existence not only at a particular time but at all times.

Expressed differently, the schema of modality is 'possibility,' i.e., a concept that is so determined that it has the possibility of existing at some moment or other. The actual is that which exists at a definite time, and the necessary is that which exists at all times.[33]

[33] "The schema of possibility is the determination of the representation of a thing at some time or other.

"The schema of actuality is existence in some determinate time.

"The schema of necessity is existence of an object at all times" (B 184).

THE SYSTEM OF ALL PRINCIPLES OF PURE UNDERSTANDING

The principles of pure understanding are judgments that are synthetic and a priori. They are judgments that are conditioned by the schematized categories. In addition to being a survey and classification of these principles, this section is also an attempt to prove the individual schematized categories.[34]

Corresponding to the schemata of quantity, quality, relation, and modality are four principles:

Axioms of Intuition

Anticipations of Perception — Analogies of Experience

Postulates of Empirical Thought

Axioms of Intuition

All that appears in experience is conditioned by its being intuited in space and time. Without space and time as a priori forms of intuition, nothing could exist in experience. But for all that exists in space and time the following principle holds: all things are extensive magnitudes.

If I imagine a line, then it is required, says Kant, that I conceive of it as drawn, i.e., as a magnitude that is formed by adding one point to another. Likewise a length of time is represented as traversed, i.e., as having come into being by one moment being added to another.[35]

[34] Cf. N. Kemp Smith, *A Commentary on Kant's Critique of Pure Reason* (New York: Humanities Press, 2nd ed. rev. 1962), p. 343 f., and Robert Paul Wolff, *Kant's Theory of Mental Activity*, p. 224.

[35] "I cannot represent to myself a line, however small, without drawing it in thought, that is, generating from a point all its parts one after another. Only in this way can the intuition be obtained. Similarly with all times, however small. In these I think to myself only that successive

Kant's assertion that we cannot conceive of a line without drawing it in our minds is misleading, because it can be understood as a psychological assertion. It can be regarded as an assertion about how our minds actually work when we imagine a line. Thus we could suppose it to mean that each time we think of a line (or any other geometrical figure) what takes place, psychologically speaking, is that first we draw it, and only when that is done do we have the notion 'line.' But this cannot be Kant's meaning. In the first place it would be a psychological assertion of doubtful validity. Few, whether they be psychologists or not, would subscribe to such a view as to how the idea of a line actually comes about. In the second place, and this is perhaps the crucial point, a psychological assertion is, from the Kantian standpoint, quite irrelevant. Kant wants to propose principles that are synthetic and a priori. A psychological assertion about how we manage to form such representations is synthetic a posteriori. There is no necessity or universal validity attached to it. Without any absurdity we could imagine other beings who formed representations in a quite different way. As a psychological assertion this would belong in the same category as, for example, the assertion that no one could construct a mental image of the letter *D* without first imagining an *A*, a *B*, and a *C*.

There is, however, a difference between saying that one cannot imagine a line without in thought drawing it and saying that one cannot conceive of a line without conceiving of it as drawn, and to conceive of it as drawn means, of course, that it is constructed by one point being added to another point and that it is therefore a synthetic unity of a manifold.

---

advance from one moment to another, whereby through the parts of time and their addition a determinate time-magnitude is generated" (B 203).

A line must always be thought of as a drawn line, and a magnitude must always be thought of as a magnitude that is constructed. Moreover, it is an a priori (and according to Kant a synthetic) proposition that a line can only be drawn or constructed and a magnitude can only come to be by a continuous process. Of course a line segment that is found printed in a geometry text book is not drawn; it is just imprinted. But the printed line is, in the last analysis, an imprint of a line that is drawn.

And so, too, with time. It is not necessary whenever I hear or use words such as 'week,' 'time,' or 'year' to run through the whole time scale to understand what I am talking about. To claim any such thing is a view so obviously absurd that scarcely anyone would subscribe to it. What, however, can be maintained as true a priori is that a period of time must always be thought of as having been formed by a continuous 'running through' of the time scale (i.e., as formed by one moment being added to another moment) and that an interval of time is a synthetic unity of a manifold.

Interpreters of Kant have often noted that there is an apparent contradiction between the Aesthetic and the Analytic (The Axioms of Intuition).[36] In the Aesthetic, space and time are not discursive concepts. They cannot be viewed as the sum of different space segments and time segments; such segments can only be thought of as segments *of* space and segments *of* time. A segment of space and a segment of time presuppose the space and time of which they are segments. Space and time precede their parts, not the other way around. But in the Axioms of Intuition Kant maintains that all magnitudes—everything that is extended in space and time—are formed by

[36] Cf. for example H. J. Paton, *Kant's Metaphysics of Experience* (New York: Humanities Press, 1936), II, 122 f. Robert Paul Wolff, *Kant's Theory of Mental Activity*, p. 229 f.

the addition of one point to another. Our understanding of anything that is extended is determined by a synthesis of a manifold. Space and time in the Analytic become discursive magnitudes.

But while the Aesthetic deals with space and time as a priori forms of intuition, as the space and time in which everything intuited necessarily must be intuited, the Analytic is concerned with the conditions for comprehending what is intuited. And the axioms of intuition deal with the conditions for comprehending the intuited as a magnitude extended in space and time. My pen is an extended thing, a magnitude, and the comprehending of it is determined by the synthetic unity of a magnitude that is itself created by the employment of the schematized category of quantity. My pen, so to say, takes up and fills out a place in space. The space in which it exists and occupies a place is the nondiscursive space of the Aesthetic. The extension that is found at, and fills, a particular place is the extensive magnitude of the axioms; it is discursive extension.

Geometry, which Kant calls the mathematics of space, is concerned with the principles of the construction of figures. The principles of the axioms of intuition, i.e., the principle that all intuitions are extensive magnitudes, is therefore basic to geometry. It is not itself an axiom from which the remaining axioms of geometry can be deduced.[37] It indicates the conditions for having a geometry at all.[38]

[37] "In the Analytic I have indeed introduced some axioms of intuition into the table of the principles of pure understanding; but the principle there applied is not itself an axiom, but serves only to specify the principle of the possibility of axioms in general and is itself no more than a principle derived from concepts" (B 761).

[38] And not necessarily Euclidian geometry. Accordingly the existence of non-Euclidian geometries does not disprove Kant. Cf. Robert Paul Wolff, *Kant's Theory of Mental Activity*, p. 231.

Anticipations of Perception

Whenever we see, hear, taste, feel, or smell something, there is a sense impression. An assertion about an existing sense impression must always be a synthetic a posteriori proposition. Whether such an assertion is true or not, only experience can confirm. Nonetheless we can, Kant believes, maintain of every assertion about an existing sense impression something that is a priori valid—something that beforehand can be said to be the case, something that can be *anticipated.*

Every sense impression has a certain degree. This is a proposition that can be asserted a priori and therefore a proposition that can be anticipated. The degree can go from zero (i.e., from the point where there is no sense impression) to any magnitude whatever. But at any given moment the sense impression has an absolutely definite degree; it has, as Kant also expresses it, a definite intensity. The degree or intensity that a given sense impression has, it has reached by increasing continually in intensity from zero up to the degree or intensity it has at the given moment. That this is the case is not an assertion that is synthetic a posteriori; often such an increase is not experienced at all. According to Kant it is a synthetic a priori proposition. This means, in other words, that it is a truth that is determined by the schematized categories of the understanding, namely by the schematized categories of 'quality.' The categories of 'quality' are, as stated previously, 'reality,' 'negation,' and 'limitation.' That they are schematized means that everything actual (every sense impression) has a definite degree (reality and limitation) and that between that degree and zero (negation) there is a continuous scale that the sense impression in question has run through.

The principle of the anticipations of perception can therefore, according to Kant, be formulated as a principle that is synthetic a priori: Whatever is real, whatever is an object of sensation, has intensive magnitude, that is, a degree.[39]

The categories under 'quantity' and 'quality' Kant calls the 'mathematical' categories, while the categories under 'relation' and 'modality' he calls the 'dynamic' categories. The axioms of intuition and the anticipations of perception are accordingly called the 'mathematical' principles, while the analogies of experience and the postulates of empirical thought are called the 'dynamic' principles. The reason for this classification is that the mathematical principles (i.e., that all objects of experience must be considered as extensive and intensive magnitude) serve as presuppositions of the different axioms of mathematics and, in addition, validate the applicability of mathematics to the objects of experience. The dynamic principles, on the other hand, have to do with the existence of objects in relation to each other (e.g., the existence of causes and effects). The mathematical principles are principles for the construction of objects; they are constitutive. The dynamic principles are presuppositions of physics; they are not principles of physics.[40]

[39] "In all appearances, the real that is an object of sensation has intensive magnitude, that is, a degree" (B 207).

[40] "The two previous principles, which, as justifying the application of mathematics to appearances, I entitled the mathematical, referred to the possibility of appearances, and taught how, alike as regards their intuition and the real in their perception, they can be generated according to rules of a mathematical synthesis. Both principles justify us in employing numerical magnitudes, and so enable us to determine appearance as magnitude. . . . It stands quite otherwise with those principles which seek to bring the *existence* of appearances under rules *a priori.* For since existence cannot be constructed, the principles can apply only to the relations of existence, and can yield only *regulative* principles. We cannot, therefore, expect either axioms or anticipations. If, however, a perception is given in a time-relation to some other perception, then even although this latter is indeterminate, and we consequently cannot decide *what* it is, or what its *magnitude* may be, we may none the less assert that in its

The Analogies of Experience

There are three analogies. The principle of the analogies is that experience is only possible where there is a necessary connection between sense perceptions.[41]

By 'experience' Kant means empirical knowledge, i.e., knowledge of an object through sense perception. Experience is a synthesis of sense impressions. It is a synthesis of a manifold, a synthesis that is the expression of the necessary unity of consciousness, an expression of transcendental apperception. Without this transcendental apperception there would be neither consciousness nor the knowledge of an object.

The categories were schematized, if we may so put it, by being brought into relationship with pure time, i.e., time as an a priori form of intuition. The category 'substance' is the means by which the synthesis of the manifold of change becomes possible. The necessity for something that is unchanged in any process of change is a synthetic judgment a priori. 'Causality' expresses an objective sequence in time; or to put the matter differently, by means of causality it is possible to create a synthesis of the manifold of succession. Finally, a synthesis of the manifold of things that exist simultaneously is possible by means of the category 'community.' The categories 'substance,' 'causality,' and 'community' are therefore the categories that are used by—and, in a certain sense, are the expression of —the three modes of time: *duration*, *succession*, and *simultaneity* (*Beharrlichkeit, Folge und Zugleichsein*).[42] It is a

---

existence it is necessarily connected with the former in this mode of time" (B 221 f.).

[41] "The principle of the analogies is: Experience is possible only through the representation of a necessary connection of perceptions" (B 218).

[42] Robert Paul Wolff maintains that Kant's categories of relation can be derived from time as the a priori form of all inner intuition: "Instead

synthetic a priori truth that there are these three modes of time and that there are no others.[43] The rules for the synthetic unity within these three modes of time are the three analogies.[44]

The First Analogy Everything exists in time. Everything is therefore a manifold of sense impressions that occur successively or of sense impressions that arise simultaneously. To say that time exists means that the two determinants of time, 'simultaneity' and 'succession,' apply to sense impressions. It

---

of beginning with the Table of Categories and hunting for time determinations, what happens if we begin with time as the form for inner sense, and try to derive a Table of Categories by analyses of time-consciousness? The answer, as we shall see in the Analogies, is that we arrive at precisely the desired categories of relation! With this simple revision, the entire Analytic suddenly falls into a perfectly logical form. Omit the Metaphysical Deduction and how does Kant's argument run?

"First, a proof that the mere fact of the unity of consciousness implies the applicability to experience of certain a priori forms of synthesis (the Deduction): then, the addition to the argument of the fact that the consciousness has a temporal form (the Schematism): lastly, the deduction of the particular forms of synthesis by an examination of the structure of the time-consciousness (the Analogies). Starting with the unity of consciousness, we arrive finally at the validity of the causal maxim. This reorganization of the Analytic diminishes somewhat the plausibility of the system of categories—those which cannot be drawn out of the time-consciousness must simply be abandoned—but it adds immeasurably to the power of the argument. Kant can be seen actually to deduce the causal maxim from the nature of subjective consciousness" (*Kant's Theory of Mental Activity*, pp. 209–10).

[43] It does not seem correct to call 'duration' (*Beharrlichkeit*) a mode of time, in any case not in the sense in which succession and simultaneity are modes of time. Kant is obviously not entirely convinced himself, for on B 226 he says: "And simultaneity and succession being the only relation in time, it follows that only in the permanent are relations of time possible. In other words, the permanent is the *substratum* of the empirical representation of time itself; in it alone is any determination of time possible" (B 226).

[44] "This *synthetic unity* in the time-relations for all perceptions, as thus determined *a priori*, is the law, that all empirical time-determinations must stand under rules of universal time-determination. The analogies of experience, with which we are now to deal, must be rules of this description" (B 220).

would have no meaning to say that simultaneity and succession apply to time itself. Kant expresses this in a misleading way when he says that time does not change.[45] It is certainly misleading as it implies that it is meaningful to say either that time does not change or that it does change, for it is clear that neither of these propositions conveys any meaning. What must be said, however, is that to speak of change is to presuppose the existence of something that does not change. This way of thinking is of long standing. Aristotle's substratum, for example, is that which remains unchanged in a process of change and without which we could not speak of change. Descartes also speaks about that which remains one and the same thing in spite of the fact that our sense impressions all change.

With Kant the argument is that a necessary condition for deciding whether something occurs earlier, later than, or simultaneously with something else is that there be something that is unchanged.[46] We may express this in a different way by saying that there must always be a subject of change. To say that there is change is to say that there is something that changes. This 'something' is the subject of the change (or, in Aristotelian language, the substratum of the change). The subject of the change is the same after the change as it was

[45] As Eduard Caird says: "It may be objected that to say that 'time' itself does not change, is like saying that passing away does not itself pass away" (*Critical Account of the Philosophy of Kant* [1. p. 541]). Quoted in N. Kemp Smith, A *Commentary to Kant's Critique of Pure Reason*, p. 359.

[46] "Our *apprehension* of the manifold of appearance is always successive, and is therefore always changing. Through it alone we can never determine whether this manifold, as object of experience, is coexistent or in sequence. For such determination we require an underlying ground which exists *at all times*, that is, something *abiding* and *permanent*, of which all change and coexistence are only so many ways (modes of time) in which the permanent exists" (B 225–26).

before the change took place. Suppose, for example, we say that thing *T* changes from being *A* to being not-*A*. *T* had the property *A* before the process began but lacks it after the process ceases. *T* is, however, still *T*. If *T* changes so that it is no longer *T*, i.e., if *T* has changed from being *T* to being *U*, this can only be expressed by saying that X has changed from being *T* to being not-*T* (namely *U*). X is then the substratum of the change—the substratum that must necessarily be presupposed.

The Second Analogy In this analogy Kant attempts to prove the principle of causality, and it is therefore in this analogy that he thinks that he has refuted Hume. What has to be proved Kant formulates as follows: "All changes take place in conformity with the law of the connection of cause and effect." [47] Or as it is expressed in the first edition: "Everything which happens (begins to happen) presupposes something which it follows in accordance with a rule." [48]

Suppose that I look at a house. I begin by looking at the chimney and the roof, and thereafter let my gaze slip down to the house's lowest story. The visual impressions come in a definite sequence. Had I begun by looking at the first floor and thereafter letting my gaze travel upward, the visual impressions would have come in the reverse sequence. The order of my sense impressions depends upon the order in which I choose to look at the house. The order is not objectively but subjectively determined. Expressed in another way, the sequence of visual impressions does not indicate that something has

[47] B 232.
[48] A 189.

happened to the house; it does not point to the occurrence or an event. From the fact that I first have the visual impressions *A* and afterwards the impressions *B*, I cannot conclude that an event took place, namely the event *A-B*.

Suppose next that I look at a ship that is sailing down a river. First I see the ship at *A* and next at *B*. That I have the visual impressions in the sequence *A-B* is not something that I choose in the same way in which I can choose to have the visual impressions of the house in a certain sequence. The sequence *A-B* in the case of the house is subjective, but in the case of the ship sailing down the river, it is objective. There I cannot have *B* before I have had *A*. The temporal order between *A* and *B* is objective, which is to say necessary. This objective and necessary sequence is the criterion of an event. The house I look at is not an event or an occurrence; it is not something that happens. The ship sailing down the river, on the other hand, is an event; it is something that takes place. The sequence of impressions with respect to the house is subjective and reversible. The sequence of sense impressions with respect to the ship sailing on the river is objective, necessary, and irreversible. It is regular and happens according to a rule. And such regularity, such a rule, is a necessary condition for being able to distinguish a subjective sequence from an objective sequence, for being able to distinguish that which is not an event from that which is.

Without such a rule, which objective (necessarily) determines the sequence of sense impressions, there would be no possibility of using concepts such as 'event' and 'occurrence'; and without this possibility, it would not be possible to make any objective judgment whatever or to have any experience (for, as Kant thought that he had shown in the transcendental deduction, the concept 'object' or 'the objective' is a necessary condition of experience).[49]

It is important to emphasize that what Kant thinks he has here proved is the principle of causality and not some empirical causal law. What is the cause of what, can only be decided by empirical observation. What is a priori certain is only that events take place according to a definite rule, but what that rule is in this or that situation must be determined a posteriori. If I see something happen or see that something has happened, I can know a priori that there is a cause (that there is, as Kant says, an event that has been followed according to a definite rule by the event that I have observed). But only experience can decide what this cause is.[50]

The Third Analogy In the second analogy Kant distinguishes between subjective temporal succession and objective temporal

[49] "If, then, my perception is to contain knowledge of an event, of something as actually happening, it must be an empirical judgment in which we think the sequence as determined; that is, it presupposes another appearance in time, upon which it follows necessarily, according to a rule. Were it not so, were I to posit the antecedent and the event were not to follow necessarily thereupon, I should have to regard the succession as a merely subjective play of my fancy; and if I still represented it to myself as something objective, I should have to call it a mere dream. Thus the relation of appearances (as possible perceptions) according to which the subsequent event, that which happens, is, as to its existence, necessarily determined in time by something preceding in conformity with a rule—in other words, the relation of cause to effect—is the condition of the objective validity of our empirical judgments, in respect of the series of perceptions, and so of their empirical truth; that is to say, it is the condition of experience. The principle of the causal relation in the sequence of appearances is therefore also valid of all objects of experience (. . . under the conditions of succession), as being itself the ground of the possibility of such experience" (B 246 f.).

[50] Regarding Hume Kant says: "Hume was therefore in error in inferring from the contingency of our determination in *accordance with the law* the contingency of the *law* itself" (B 794).

succession. The sequence of sense impressions in the case of the house is subjective, while the sequence of sense impressions in the case of the ship sailing down the river is objective. The subjective sequence does not constitute an event, but the objective sequence does. The difference between the subjective and the objective sequences shows itself also in the fact that the one is reversible while the other is not.

If there is a causal relationship between two events *A* and *B*, then A exists before *B*. A and *B* cannot exist simultaneously. The condition for saying that two things exist at one and the same time is that the sequence of sensations is reversible. To be able to speak of coexistence, the sense impressions must be sense impressions of an object. What can be said to coexist when the sense impressions are reversible is not the sense impressions themselves but that of which the sense impressions are sense impressions. I have a sense impression of the roof and then a sense impression of the basement; what exist simultaneously are the roof and the basement, not the sense impression of the roof and the sense impression of the basement. I have a sense impression of the moon and a sense impression of the earth. The sequence of these two sense impressions is reversible, but the moon and the earth coexist.

All things that exist simultaneously stand in a reciprocal relationship. This is what Kant maintains in the third analogy,[51] and it is what he seeks to prove.

A ship that is sailing down the river and is first at *A* and next at *B* cannot again be seen at *A*, provided we assume that it continues sailing in the same direction. Should the sequence suddenly be reversible, so that besides being able to see it at

[51] "All substances, in so far as they can be perceived to coexist in space, are in thoroughgoing reciprocity" (B 256). In the first edition this reads, "All substances, so far as they coexist, stand in thoroughgoing community, that is, in mutual interaction" (A 211).

B or *C*, I am again able to see it at *A*, then I must conclude either that it was an optical illusion or that it actually was not the same ship at all. What I was confronted with was not one ship but two—ships that were on the river simultaneously at A and *B* (or *C*). If in addition I should convince myself that it actually was two simultaneously existing ships, I might then let my gaze go from one to the other. I might assure myself of the matter by ascertaining that the sequence of sense impressions was reversible. But to say that the sequence was reversible would simply mean that a causal relationship was not at issue. The roof is not the cause of the basement, and the basement is not the cause of the roof. And yet while it certainly would be nonsense to maintain that the roof was the cause of the basement or that the basement was the cause of the roof, it is not nonsense (in any case Kant does not think that it is) to maintain that there is a reciprocal relationship between them, i.e., that the roof is dependent upon (is an effect of) the basement at the same time that the basement is dependent upon (is an effect of) the roof. In other words, if a sequence of sense impressions is not reversible, a causal relationship is present. If, on the other hand, the sequence is reversible, i.e., if I, at my convenience, can begin with A and then go to *B* or begin with *B* and go to A, then it is a question of a relationship of interaction; such a reciprocal relationship indicates simultaneity (coexistence).

That sense impressions follow one another in accordance with a rule is, according to Kant's second analogy, the same as saying that there exists a causal relationship. And if the sequence is reversible, then there is a rule that allows me to go from *A* to *B* and a rule that allows me to go from *B* to *A*, or, in other words, regardless of whether I go the one way or the other, the course of the sense impressions is regular. There is therefore a mutual causal relationship: there is a reciprocal relationship.

Suppose that this were not the case; suppose that the different things or substances existed independently of each other, that they were wholly isolated. In that case it would be impossible to discover that something ever exists simultaneously with (or before or after) something else. This, at least, is what Kant maintains. In other words, I would not be able to conclude from a sequence of sense impressions and its possible reversibility that they were sense impressions of things that existed at one and the same moment.

A temporal sequence is objective when it is objectively determined, i.e., is determined by a rule or law. Objective temporal sequence (succession) is an expression of causality. Objective simultaneity does not express causality. For if A is the cause of *B*, A and *B* do not exist simultaneously. What is here required, according to Kant, is that *A* is dependent on *B*, that *B* acts on *A*, and also that *B* is dependent on *A* and that A acts on *B*. In other words there must be reciprocity between A and *B*.

The analogies are principles for the synthesis of the manifold with respect to time. They are principles that are determined not by experience but by pure apperception; they set the conditions of experience. Substance, causality, and interaction (reciprocity) are necessary conditions for creating a unity with respect to what Kant calls the three modes of time: duration, succession, and simultaneity. Since these three modes are necessary conditions of experience, the principles that determine them—i.e., set the conditions under which we are able to speak of duration, succession, and simultaneity—are likewise necessary conditions of experience. And the conditions for creating a unity with respect to duration, succession, and simultaneity are substance, causality, and interaction (reciprocity). Substance, causality, and reciprocity are, in other words, the conditions of experience. If by nature we understand the connection of things that exist, and if, furthermore, everything exists in time, then it follows that the analogies determine nature. For it is the analogies that determine this connection. The various empirical laws, whose validity is verified through experience, are thus only possible by virtue of the a priori condition of experience that the analogies provide.[52]

The Postulates of Empirical Thought

The First Postulate The postulates are not principles regarding the conditions of experience. They indicate the conditions under which something can be considered as possible, actual, or necessary. Or, if one will, they clarify what is to be understood by the modal concepts 'possibility,' 'actuality,' and 'necessity.'

The first postulate states that the possible is that which agrees with the formal conditions of experience.[53]

This definition of the possible is different, for example, from Leibniz's. According to Leibniz, whatever is free of contradiction is possible. The criterion of possible existence is

[52] "By nature, in the empirical sense, we understand the connection of appearances as regards their existence according to necessary rules, that is, according to laws. There are certain laws which first make a nature possible, and these laws are *a priori*. Empirical laws can exist, and be discovered only through experience, and indeed in consequence of those original laws through which experience itself first becomes possible. Our analogies therefore really portray the unity of nature in the connection of all appearances under certain exponents which express nothing save the relation of time (in so far as time comprehends all existence) to the unity of apperception—such unity being possible only in synthesis according to rules. Taken together, the analogies thus declare that all appearances lie, and must lie, in *one* nature, because without this *a priori* unity no unity of experience, and therefore no determination of objects in it, would be possible" (B 263).

[53] "That which agrees with the formal conditions of experience, that is, with the conditions of intuition and of concepts, is *possible*" (B 265).

freedom from contradiction. But for Kant freedom from contradiction is not enough. In order that a concept can have the possibility of existence, it must in addition be in agreement with the conditions of experience—i.e., it must agree with the axioms of intuition, the anticipations of perception, and the analogies of experience.[54]

To say that something is a possibility in the sense in which the concept 'possibility' has to be understood according to the first postulate, is to say that it is an empirical possibility. It is a possibility in the sense in which I can, for example, say that it is possible that oil exists in Denmark's subsoil. This indicates that I think that there is some evidence for it, but that I am not certain of my position. If it turns out that no oil is found, then in the sense in which Kant here takes the word, this is the same as saying that obviously it was not a possibility. And if oil is found, then I say that obviously it not only was a possibility, it is also actually the case. I can believe that something is a possibility and mean thereby that I am unable to decide whether in fact it is or is not possible. This Kantian meaning of the concept is different from the meaning the concept often has. According to this latter meaning I can, for example, say that the existence of a golden mountain is a possibility. Such a supposition is not a contradiction (as would be, for example, the supposition of the existence of a round square). A golden mountain is, to be sure, an object that we

[54] Kant's formulation of the first postulate might suggest that he did not think that only that which is in accordance with the conditions of experience is possible. Just because being in agreement with the conditions of experience implies being possible, it does not follow that what is possible entails being in accordance with the conditions of experience. That Kant thinks that only what is in agreement with the conditions of experience is possible follows, however, from what he says in B 267: "The postulate of the *possibility* of things requires that the concept of the things should agree with the formal conditions of an experience in general."

know very well does not exist but that we are nonetheless readily able to imagine as existing. But according to Kant's view, the fact that no such mountain is found proves that it is not possible. But so long as we are without empirical evidence pro or con, we can believe that its existence is a possibility.

The Second Postulate The difference between possibility and actuality is a question of sense impression. As long as something is not verified, i.e., is not established in experience, it cannot be considered as actual. The criterion for something to be actual is that it appears as, or can be connected with, sense perception.[55]

The determination of something as actual does not require that it appear as a sense perception or a sense impression. Whether or not something is actual does not depend upon the effectiveness of our sense organs. It is sufficient that it would exist as a sense impression were our sense organs sufficiently sharp. From a particular sense perception we can often, by means of certain empirical laws, infer the existence of something that does not itself appear as a sense impression but would do so if our sense organs were keen enough.[56] The second postulate thus expresses the empirical thesis that knowledge of a concept is never sufficient grounds to warrant our concluding that this concept is of something actual. Only sense perception can decide what is actual.

[55] Kant formulates the second postulate in this way: "That which is bound up with the material conditions of experience, that is, with sensation, is actual" (B 266).

[56] "Thus from the perception of the attracted iron filings we know of the existence of a magnetic matter pervading all bodies, although the constitution of our organs cuts us off from all immediate perception of this medium" (B 273).

The Third Postulate If I see some water boiling, this is a sign of something actual, and this is just what the second postulate says. If in addition I can establish that the water is boiling as a consequence of the fact that it has been heated to 212°, then I have established that what exists (the boiling water) is something that necessarily will occur when and where these conditions are present.[57] One consequence of the second analogy appears to be that everything that is actual is also necessary. Everything occurs according to determinate law, and everything must therefore be necessary. The difference between the actual and the necessary is consequently epistemological—it is a distinction with respect to our knowledge of the existing thing. That something appears as a sense perception merely entitles us to call it actual. Only when something is recognized to be an event that can be deduced by means of a particular empirical law is it recognized as necessary. But even if some existing thing is not known to be necessary, we can by virtue of the second analogy know a priori that it can be known to be necessary. Everything that occurs is both actual and necessary. It is actual *qua* sense perception; it is necessary *qua* the natural law, by means of which it can be calculated in advance.

But it is not only the actual that is merged with the necessary. A further consequence of Kant's view of the three modal concepts is that the possible coincides also with both the actual and the necessary.[58] There is nothing in this world that is not

[57] The third postulate he formulates as follows: "That which in its connection with the actual is determined in accordance with universal conditions of experience, is (that is, exist as) *necessary*" (B 266).

[58] "Everything actual is possible; from this proposition there naturally follows, in accordance with the logical rules of conversion, the merely particular proposition, that some possible is actual; and this would seem to mean that much is possible which is not actual. It does indeed seem as if we were justified in extending the number of possible things beyond that of the actual, on the ground that something must be added to the pos-

at one and the same time possible, actual, and necessary. The condition for saying that a particular thing is either possible, actual, or necessary depends upon the degree of our knowledge of its connections with other things. If I am asked whether we will have sunshine on Sunday, I may answer that it is possible and may mean thereby that I do not have sufficient knowledge of weather conditions to be able to say that it either will or will not be sunny. If on Sunday I discover that it actually is sunny, then it is thereby an established fact. And if I had had sufficient knowledge of the laws of meteorology, then by these laws I would have been able to see why it necessarily had to be sunny.

Kant's Refutation of Idealism As a special section under the postulates of empirical thought Kant adds his famous *Widerlegung des Idealismus*, in which he distinguishes between problematic and dogmatic idealism. By problematic idealism he means the hypothesis that the existence of spatial objects is either doubtful or incapable of proof, an idealism he ascribes to Descartes. Dogmatic idealism, on the other hand, assumes that the existence of space and thereby of spatial objects is an impossibility. This form of idealism Kant attributes to Berkeley. Against these two forms of idealism Kant maintains that we directly experience external objects, and he seeks to prove this by showing that such experience is a necessary presupposition of self-consciousness (the self-consciousness that is the starting point of problematic idealism).[59]

---

sible to constitute the actual. But this (alleged) process of adding to the possible I refuse to allow. For that which would have to be added to the possible, over and above the possible, would be impossible" (B 283 f.).

[59] Kant's thesis reads as follows: "The mere, but empirically determined, consciousness of my own existence proves the existence of objects in space outside me" (B 275).

I am conscious of my own existence, an existence that is going on in time. This is an empirical self-consciousness. As we have seen in the first analogy, every determination of time requires not only change but also something that does not change (*etwas Beharrliches*). Change only has meaning when we have a criterion for determining what has not changed. Empirical self-consciousness is constituted by a continuous flux of representations; the life of consciousness is a succession of various phenomena of consciousness (cf. William James's expression, 'the stream of consciousness'). In order that I can know my own consciousness, which I experience as a flux of representations, something unchanging is required. But this unchanging element, by means of which I recognize my consciousness as my own, I cannot find in myself. Therefore it must be found outside of me. It can only be found in those objects that are intuited in space, as Kant argued in the first analogy.

Kant does not apply the schematized category of substance to self-consciousness. The unchanging that he would in that case have to presuppose would be the transcendental apperception, which he claims is not a substance. The transcendental apperception is the presupposition of all categories and can therefore not be subsumed under any one of them.[60]

Descartes began with a *cogito* and thought that he could derive from it the existence of the external world. Kant thinks that the fact that there is a *cogito* is itself only possible under the condition that there is direct experience of the external world. We experience external objects immediately and directly. Space and thereby the external world have objective existence. It can hardly be said more explicitly than Kant here states it, that space and that which is experienced in space are not subjective but in all respects objective. Kant is, as he him-

[60] Cf. A. C. Ewing, *A Short Commentary on Kant's Critique of Pure Reason* (London: Methuen & Co., Ltd., 1961), p. 151.

self puts it, an empirical realist. True, he also calls himself a transcendental idealist. What he means by this second designation will be discussed later.

PHENOMENA AND NOUMENA

Time and time again in *The Critique of Pure Reason* Kant emphasizes that the categories are only applicable to what is given in space and time. The categories have empirical but not transcendent applicability. We cannot therefore understand something as a transcendent object—i.e., an object that does not appear in space and time.

But from the fact that we call what is intuited in space and time 'phenomena,' then it follows that it must be meaningful to speak of that which is not phenomenon and which Kant calls the thing-in-itself or 'noumenon.' [61] But here, according to Kant, there lies a danger. For to make a concept of a noumenon already presupposes the employment of the categories. We cannot understand anything, we cannot form any thought or any concept except by means of categories. And the categories, as has just been emphasized, cannot be employed transcendently but only empirically. The danger thus lies in thinking that we can form a concept of a noumenon, which according to critical philosophy is something that just cannot be done.

Kant distinguishes therefore between a negative and a positive meaning of the concept 'noumenon.' In its negative meaning the concept 'noumenon' is not an object of intuition. In

[61] "At the very outset, however, we come upon an ambiguity which may occasion serious misapprehension. The understanding, when it entitles an object in a (certain) relation mere phenomenon, at the same time forms, apart from that relation, a representation of an *object in itself* and so comes to represent itself as also being able to form *concepts* of such objects" (B 306 f.).

the positive meaning of the concept, 'noumenon' means an object that can be intuited through a special kind of nonsensory intuition. Kant rejects the positive meaning of the concept, not because it is meaningless, but because it presupposes a kind of intuition that he claims we do not possess.[62] This argument is, however, not purely epistemological or logical but rather psychological: had we been another kind of beings, which had a different kind of intuition, namely a nonsensory intuition, then we would have had the possibility of intuiting such objects. If, however, we accept an epistemological or logical interpretation of *The Critique of Pure Reason,* which Kant in fact requires us to do, we must insist that the concept 'intuition' only has meaning when it is understood in the way in which Kant defines it in the Aesthetic. But whatever logical status the concept 'noumenon' may have in its positive meaning, it is in any case rejected by Kant, for he acknowledges only the negative meaning. The concept 'noumenon' is thus not a concept of some sensible object or other, but is a concept of something that is not an object that can be perceived by the senses—which is the same as saying that it is not a concept of any object at all.

To classify objects as empirical and transcendental respectively (phenomena and noumena), is therefore, according to Kant, a misunderstanding; such a division would presuppose that the concept 'noumenon' had been taken in the positive sense. Kant's view of noumena is thus quite different, for example, from Locke's view of the external object. According to Locke the external object is precisely an object, although it is

[62] "But if we understand by it an *object* of a *non-sensible intuition,* we thereby presuppose a special mode of intuition, and of which we cannot comprehend even the possibility. This would be 'noumenon' in the *positive* sense of the term" (B 307).

an object about which we cannot know anything other than that it has primary qualities that are numerically different from the primary ideas, although they are qualitatively identical with them.

If, however, it is impermissible or even meaningless to assume the existence of two kinds of objects, it is nonetheless permissible, even necessary, to have the *concept* noumenon, namely as a concept that limits what is intuited in space and time, as that which sets limits to what can be *intuited* and therefore known.[63]

THE AMPHIBOLY OF CONCEPTS OF REFLECTION

In this section (or *Anhang*, as Kant calls it) Kant turns to the Leibnizian philosophy and attempts to point out the errors on which it rests. There are four aspects of this philosophy that Kant examines: (1) identity and difference; (2) agreement and opposition; (3) the inner and the outer; (4) matter and form.

Leibniz's error, according to Kant, is that he overlooks the significance of sensation for knowledge. For Kant both *Verstand* and *Sinnlichkeit* are necessary for knowledge; they are what he calls, perhaps somewhat infelicitously, the two *Erkenntnisquellen, Erkenntnisvermögen, Erkenntniskräfte* or *Erkenntnisarten*—infelicitously, not only because they are psychological expressions and therefore contrary to the epistemological point of view found in *The Critique of Pure Reason,* but also because

[63] "The concept of a noumenon is thus a merely *limiting concept*, the function of which is to curb the pretensions of sensibility; and it is therefore only of negative employment. At the same time it is no arbitrary invention; it is bound up with the limitation of sensibility, though it cannot affirm anything positive beyond the field of sensibility" (B 310 f.).

they give the impression that we can gain knowledge either through the understanding alone or through sensation alone, a view that Kant vigorously opposes.

Kant criticizes Leibniz for deducing judgments concerning reality from concepts alone, without relying on sensation. Kant expresses the Leibnizian error formally as follows: Leibniz does not content himself with the accepted use of the principle *Dictum de omni et nullo;* he uses it also, so to speak, in a negative way. It is correct to maintain that what holds for everything within a certain class holds also for every single member of that class. But we have, of course, no right to conclude that because a given predicate does not belong to every member of a certain class, it does not belong to any members of that class. Kant expresses the principle in this way: that which universally agrees with, or contradicts, a concept also agrees with, or contradicts, everything that is included under this concept; while the negative principle, the principle he rejects, is expressed in this fashion: that which does not belong to a concept does not belong to that which is included under this concept either.[64]

It is true of all birds that they have wings, lay eggs, and breathe with their lungs. This is therefore also true of the particular bird at which I happen now to be looking. But from

[64] "It is indeed true that whatever universally agrees with or contradicts a concept also agrees with or contradicts every particular which is contained under it (dictum de omni et nullo) but it would be absurd to alter this logical principle so as to read: what is not contained in a universal concept is also not included in the particular concepts which stand under it. For these are particular concepts just because they include in themselves more than is thought in the universal. Nevertheless it is upon this latter principle that the whole intellectual system of Leibniz is based; and with this principle it therefore falls, together with all the ambiguities (in the employment of the understanding) that have thence arisen" (B 337).

the fact that it is not true of all birds that they are black, we cannot conclude that it is not true of some birds.

One of Leibniz's metaphysical principles is the principle of the identity of what does not have different characteristics. It is the well-known *principium identitatis indiscernibilium.* One cannot have a concept of two things that in all respects are identical (i.e., two things that are only numerically different). That two things are numerically different means that they are located at different places in space. The book that is lying in front of me is only one book; it is numerically identical with itself. At the bookstore there are ten copies of the same book. These ten copies are all identical, but they are numerically different. According to Leibniz there cannot be any two things that in all respects are identical and yet numerically different. Numerical difference implies in addition a difference with respect to the predicates that belong to the two things.

This principle is in part a consequence of another of Leibniz's principles, the so-called *in esse* principle. In every true judgment the predicate only predicates something that could have been known a priori if we had had a complete knowledge of the subject's concept. Certainly it is through experience that we have learned, for example, that water freezes at 32° F., but this is because it is not possible for us to learn to know the concept 'water' in any other way. Had we had sufficient knowledge about the nature of water, we would have known that the predicate 'freezes at 32° F.' follows from the concept itself. This relationship holds for individual concepts also. Leibniz goes so far as to maintain that he who had a perfect knowledge of, for example, the concept 'Alexander the Great' (what Leibniz calls Alexander's *haecceitas*) would also be able to know a priori what can truly be predicated about Alexander, including everything that Alexander thought, said, and did and everything that happened to him—whether, for example, he died a natural death or was poisoned.[65] If every concept is unambiguously determined through each and every predicate that belongs to it, then it follows, according to Leibniz, that two things cannot be different merely with respect to their location in space. Every individual is an individual by being a distinct individual and not some other individual; and it is a distinct individual by virtue of what characterizes it, by the predicates that can be predicated of it. There cannot therefore be two things that have exactly the same predicates.[66]

The concept of a cubic foot is a concept that is identical with itself; it is always one and the same. But two cubic feet that exist in two different places in space are, Kant maintains, necessarily also identical except for the fact that they are numerically different. Space and time—the necessary presuppositions of intuition—are also presuppositions for two things being numerically different, in spite of the fact that they are entirely identical. The concept 'cubic foot' does not permit us to think of two numerically different cubic feet. As sense objects, as intuitions, there can, however, be infinitely many identical but numerically different cubic feet.

No concept can contain determinations that are mutually in conflict. Such determinations will cancel each other and therefore also cancel the concept. A predicate either can be predicated of a concept or it cannot. The alternative is a logical contradiction, which neither Leibniz nor Kant could accept. However, Kant distinguishes, as Leibniz does not, be-

[65] Cf. Leibniz, *Nouveaux Essais*, XXVII, Secs. 1–3, *Discours de Metaphysique* VIII. Cf. also Leibniz's letter to Count Ernst von Hessen-Rheinfels of April 12, 1686.

[66] Leibniz also used the principle of sufficient reason as support for his *principium identitatis indiscernibilium*.

tween a concept and objects of experience (i.e., objects in space and time). Furthermore, it is possible to find objects (not concepts) of which we can predicate conflicting determinations—but not, be it noted, propositions that contradict each other logically. For example, two forces that are directed against each other can act on a body with the result that they cancel each other. Also with respect to this point, therefore, Leibniz's mistake is, so Kant thinks, that he does not acknowledge spatial and temporal intuition, or what is the same, acknowledge experience as a necessary condition for knowledge.

The difference between the inner and the outer is that the outer is in space while the inner is not. That which is an outer object (substance) is therefore an object to which such predicates as determination of place, magnitude, touch, and movement must necessarily belong. No such determinations can be attributed to what is denoted as inner. If we take all of the determinations of space away, the inner (the inner substance) can only be determined as a state of consciousness, and the inner substance (the monads of Leibniz) possesses then no powers other than the powers to form perceptions.

The crucial difference between the viewpoints of Kant and Leibniz here stands out clearly. For Leibniz space, understood as something extended, is not real, and sensation is not the way to truth. Knowledge is to be reached through reason and not through sense perception. Sense perception gives only an unreliable and unclear picture of what reason can see clearly and correctly. If one is to obtain knowledge of the true nature of reality (of what exists, i.e., substance), one must therefore disregard extension and sensation. The result is necessarily the monad. Kant's position is quite different. For him space is empirically real. Intuition is a necessary condition of knowledge and therefore plays an independent role. To ignore the empirical reality of space is to ignore that which is necessary for knowledge, and the result can only be erroneous.

By matter and form Kant means the possible and the actualized, or to use Kant's own expression, that which is to be determined (*das Bestimmbare*) and its determination (*die Bestimmung*). From the meaning of these concepts one may infer that matter (the possible, or that which is not yet determined) must have logical priority: form presupposes matter. And matter, i.e., that which is to be determined, is according to Leibniz the monads. Space is a determination of the monads' mutual relation[67]—i.e., a determination that presupposes the monads. For Kant, on the other hand, space is the form of intuition, and the form of intuition presupposes the matter of intuition (sense impressions).

[67] Cf. Leibniz's fifth letter to Clarke, 47.

4) *The Transcendental Dialectic*

THE TRANSCENDENTAL ILLUSION

The Transcendental Logic has two parts: the Transcendental Analytic and Transcendental Dialectic. In the Transcendental Analytic Kant attempts to show that there are categories and that the categories are necessary conditions of knowledge; also that they are only applicable to what is given in intuition. In the Transcendental Dialectic he argues that it is the nature of reason to employ the categories beyond that which is given in space and time and thereby to pose and to try to answer metaphysical questions. But even if these metaphysical questions are an expression of the essence of reason, they are nonetheless illegitimate. As Kant time and again emphasizes, the categories can only be applied to what is intuited, and an offense against this rule results in what he calls a transcendental illusion. But since a transcendental illusion has its roots in the essence of reason, it is unavoidable. It can be recognized as an illusion, but it can be eliminated as little as an optical illusion can be eliminated by knowing that it is an illusion. A stick that appears broken in water does so whether or not we understand that it is not really broken.

Kant distinguishes between understanding and reason. To think an object, i.e., make a judgment about what is given in space and time so that by means of categories it becomes a judgment about an object, is an activity of the understanding. In other words, the activity of the understanding consists in creating by means of categories a unity of the manifold that is given in space and time. And since in the last analysis the categories are conditioned by transcendental apperception, the activity of the understanding reflects just this apperception.

Judgments can enter into a syllogism as premises. To draw conclusions is an activity of reason. Just as Kant thought that he could discover the categories by considering the logical form of the different judgments, so also he thinks that he can find what he calls 'the ideas of reason' by considering the different forms of inference. Kant takes for granted the three traditional forms of inference: the categorical, the hypothetical, and the disjunctive. To each of these forms of inference one of the three ideas of reason corresponds. To the categorical form of inference corresponds the idea 'soul'; to the hypothetical, the idea 'world'; and to the disjunctive, the idea 'God.'

Let us take the categorical form of inference (syllogism). It consists of three categorical judgments of which two are premises and the third is the conclusion. Kant's example (cf. B 360) is as follows:

1. All men are mortal
2. All scholars are men

---

3. All scholars are mortal

(1) is the major premise. Kant characterizes this as a rule. (2) is the minor premise, in which the concept 'scholar' is subsumed under the concept 'man.' The rule expressed in the major premise holds true therefore of all scholars. (3) is the result of applying this rule to the concept 'scholar.' A syllogism is thus a matter of judgments and concepts. The validity of the judgments is shown subject to the validity of certain other judgments and by the concepts being subsumed under each other.

Such an activity is completely different from the activity of the understanding. By means of the categories, the understanding creates in a judgment a unity out of the manifold that is given in intuition. Reason attempts to create a unity by bringing as many concepts and thereby as many judgments as possible under a general rule. The rule, "All men are mortal," is one that includes not only the judgment, "All scholars are men," but also innumerable others, namely all to whose subject the predicate 'man' belongs.

If it is the activity of reason to bring judgments under a general rule so that certain judgments can be said to follow from certain others by virtue of this rule, then reason must necessarily also seek to bring every major premise under a new rule by virtue of which it follows as a conclusion. In order to deduce the major premise in the foregoing syllogism—i.e., the judgment, "All men are mortal"—we can, for example, pose the major premise, "All animals are mortal," and thus get the following syllogism (prosyllogism):

1. All animals are mortal
2. All men are animals

---

3. All men are mortal

We can express this by saying that reason seeks the conditions of the conditions; it seeks that which conditions all that is conditioned; in other words, it seeks the unconditioned.[1] This is the principle of pure reason. Such a principle is, of course, transcendent. The categories of the understanding permit only what is conditioned. It is obviously a truism to maintain that the conditioned has a condition; but it is not a truism to maintain that the series of conditions can be brought to completion, or in other words that the unconditioned exists. It is a synthetic proposition that neither is applied nor can be applied to the empirical in the way in which the principles of the Analytic can and necessarily must be.

If we consider the foregoing syllogism, we see that in the conclusion the predicate 'mortal' is predicated of the class of all men, while in the major premise it is predicated of the class of all animals, i.e., of a class that is of larger compass than (and includes) the class of all men. The next major premise, the one by virtue of which the judgment, "All animals are mortal," can be deduced, might be, "All organisms are mortal." If then we have the judgment, "All animals are organisms," as the minor premise, the conclusion follows, "All animals are mortal." In order to be able to deduce the judgment, "All animals are mortal," it is not enough, as we see, to have the major premise, "All organisms are mortal"; we must also have the minor premise, "All animals are organisms." The subject in the major premise must be able to serve as the predicate in the minor premise. If we should therefore come upon a subject in the major premise that cannot be a predicate,

[1] "Now since this rule is itself subject to the same requirement of reason, and the condition of the condition must therefore be sought (by means of a prosyllogism) whenever practicable, obviously the principle peculiar to reason in general, in its logical employment, is: to find for the conditioned knowledge obtained through the understanding the unconditioned whereby its unity is brought to completion" (B 364).

the continuation of the prosyllogisms would be rendered impossible.[2]

While the understanding *qua* the categories of the understanding is concerned with the conditioned and relative, the goal of reason, as already mentioned, is necessarily the unconditioned and the absolute. To recognize something as conditioned already presupposes the idea of the unconditioned. It is meaningless to speak of something conditioned unless we have the concept of the unconditioned. The concepts of the conditioned and the unconditioned, the relative and the absolute, the uncompleted and the completed, are polar concepts, which for that reason logically presuppose each other. To know that a syllogism, a hypothetical inference or a disjunctive inference is conditioned, is to presuppose the idea of the absolute condition of such inferences. Reason thus appears necessarily to arrive at metaphysical ideas: at the completed, the unconditioned, and the absolute.

The three ideas of the unconditioned and the absolute are formed through the three forms of inference. Through the categorical syllogism the idea of the absolute subject (the soul) is formed. Through the hypothetical form of inference is formed the idea of the absolute unity of the conditions of that which appears in experience (the world); and finally, through the disjunctive form of inference comes the idea of the absolute unity of the conditions of everything that can be thought.[3]

[2] Kant maintains, however, that such a series can be continued indefinitely: "Now every series the exponent of which is given (in categorical or hypothetical judgment) can be continued; consequently this same activity of reason leads to *ratiocinatio polysyllogistica*, which is a series of inferences that can be prolonged indefinitely on the side either of the conditions (*per prosyllogismos*) or of the conditioned (*per episyllogismos*)" (B 387 f.).

[3] "All transcendental ideas can therefore be arranged in three classes,

The metaphysical discipline that has as its object the thinking subject is what Kant calls rational psychology. Cosmology has the world as object, and theology has God.[4]

Since there is nothing empirical that corresponds to these ideas, it is impossible for the understanding to form for itself any picture of the objects of the metaphysical disciplines here referred to. Kant calls the ideas transcendental; for the uncompleted and the conditioned require the idea of the completed and the unconditioned. It would be impossible for the uncompleted and the conditioned to strive toward the completed and the unconditioned if the idea of the unconditioned did not exist. If the uncompleted attained completion, there would no longer be any need for an idea of the completed; for the inference from the condition to the conditioned is not the business of reason but of the understanding. The transcendent ideas serve only as conditions of making inferences from the conditioned to the unconditioned.[5]

---

the *first* containing the absolute (unconditioned) *unity* of the *thinking subject*, the *second* the absolute *unity of the series of conditions of appearance*, the *third* the absolute *unity of the condition of all objects of thought in general*" (B 391).

[4] "Subsequently, the attempt was made to subordinate this given matter to the schema of the transcendental logic. As the Dialectic is construed as the doctrine of the syllogism, these disciplines, likewise, must submit to being brought by all kinds of artifices under the viewpoint of the categorical, hypothetical, and disjunctive syllogism. That this is all the idle play of a capricious scholastic subtlety, needs no elaboration" (Friedrich Paulsen, *Immanuel Kant, His Life and Doctrine*, trans. from the rev. German ed. by J. E. Creighton and Albert Lefevre [New York: Chas. Scribner's Sons, 1902], p. 212).

[5] As Kant expresses it: "As easily seen, what pure reason alone has in view is the absolute totality of the synthesis *on the side of the conditions* (whether of inherence, of dependence, or of concurrence); it is not concerned with absolute completeness *on the side of the conditioned.* For the former alone is required in order to presuppose the whole series of the conditions, and to present it *a priori* to the understanding. Once we are given a complete (and unconditioned) condition, no concept of reason is required for the continuation of the series; for every step in the

But even if there is not and cannot be any concept of an idea as an object, we are nonetheless led through what Kant characterizes as a sophism (in contradistinction to a rational inference) to assume the objective reality of the idea. There are three kinds of such inferences: (1) paralogisms (inferences concerning the idea of a soul); (2) antinomies (inferences concerning the idea of the world); and (3) the idea of pure reason (inferences concerning the idea of God).

THE PARALOGISMS OF PURE REASON

There are two kinds of paralogisms, logical and transcendental paralogisms. A logical paralogism is a syllogism in which a formal logical mistake has been made. We have, for example, a logical paralogism in the following syllogism:

1. Journalists are good writers
2. Authors of short stories are good writers

---

3. Journalists are authors of short stories

A transcendental paralogism is an erroneous syllogism in which the error is not of a formal nature but is to be found in the nature of reason itself. In contradistinction to the error in the logical paralogism, it is an error that reason cannot avoid even though, when suitably instructed, it can avoid being led astray by it—in the same way in which we cannot avoid an optical illusion, but suitably instructed, we can avoid being led astray by it.

forward direction from the condition to the *conditioned* is carried through by the understanding itself. The transcendental ideas thus serve only for *ascending,* in the series of conditions, to the unconditioned, that is, to principles" (B 393).

The foundation of the transcendental paralogisms is pure apperception. As will be remembered, Kant maintains (B 131 f.) that every thought or act of consciousness must be a thought or act of consciousness on the part of an "I." It must always be possible for an "I think" to accompany every act of consciousness. There must thus be an 'I' for every thought or act of consciousness that exists. This "I think" is an expression of the transcendental unity of consciousness, the unity that is a condition of all consciousness and therefore cannot itself be an object of consciousness. This pure consciousness, the transcendental unity of consciousness, this pure or transcendental apperception, the transcendental 'I,' is not a possible object of knowledge, for this would presuppose the employment of categories. But the use of categories presupposes pure apperception; consequently they cannot be applied to it. (Compare: a presupposition for my seeing is that I have eyes. My eyes, with which I see, cannot therefore be among the objects that I see.)

The First Paralogism

Rational psychology, which according to Kant is a consequence of the transcendental paralogism, has its basis in the "I think" of transcendental apperception.

Every application of the categories to the subject of the judgment, "I think," is, as has just been emphasized, a transcendental error. Every determination of thought of this 'I,' every statement about it, constitutes a transgression of the limits of the proper use of categories. If it is said of this 'I' that it is a substance, the first step upon the path of rational psychology has been taken. Kant states the paralogism thus (B 410 f.):

1. That which cannot be viewed as other than subject exists only as subject and is therefore a substance.
2. A thinking being (an 'I') cannot be comprehended as anything other than subject (it cannot meaningfully be predicated of something).

---

3. A thinking being (an 'I') therefore exists as a substance.

The form of the syllogism is 'Barbara' and is therefore apparently valid. A presupposition of there being a syllogism is that there are only three terms, the major, the minor, and the middle terms. If that which is considered as being the middle term proves to have one meaning in the major premise and another in the minor premise, then it is no longer a question of three concepts but of four (*quaternio terminorum*), and the result is a so-called *sophisma figurae dictionis*. According to Kant, the above syllogism is precisely a *sophisma figurae dictionis,* since the middle term signifies something different in each of the two premises. In both premises the word 'subject' is used, but in each (according to Kant) it means something different. In the major premise it means 'a thinking subject,' i.e., a subject about which a judgment can be made, a subject about which something can be asserted, a subject, therefore, that can be thought of as an object that is given in space and time. In the minor premise, on the other hand, the word means something that cannot be thought of as an object given in space and time, since it is the condition of anything being thought at all.

Kant concludes, therefore, that there can be no knowledge of a subject that cannot itself be a predicate. We have no possibility of proving that such a concept has objective reality.

That the paralogism is transcendental and not simply logical follows from the fact that it is the nature of reason to look at every subject as a name of an object—the object of which the predicate predicates something. The predicate is predicated of that which the subject names. But to regard the grammatical subject in the judgment "I think" as a name of some kind of object or being of which the predicate 'think' is predicated is to make a transcendental error.

The Second Paralogism

The second paralogism has to do with the 'I' (soul) as simple. The paralogism has the following premises:[6]

1. That of which the actions cannot be regarded as a concurrence of several things acting is simple.
2. This relation holds true of the soul (the thinking 'I').

---

3. The soul is simple.

A machine's performance is often the result of several different things, whose various different functions are so combined as to result in exactly what the machine does at any particular moment. Several different men can each write down a line of a given verse, and the result is the whole verse. But if several different men each imagine a line of the verse, the result is not a representation of the whole verse.

The nerve of the proof (*nervus probandi*) is, according to Kant, that the absolute unity of the thinking subject must necessarily be presupposed in order that the combination of various representations can form one thought.[7]

That which is presupposed is accordingly pure apperception, and the proposition "I think" is only an expression of this

[6] A 351.
[7] "The so-called *nervus probandi* of this argument lies in the proposition, that if a multiplicity of representations are to form a single representation, they must be contained in the absolute unity of the thinking subject" (A 352).

apperception. Apperception is the presupposition of having and using concepts, and is therefore not itself a concept.[8] It is consequently a misunderstanding to attempt to arrive at any knowledge of this thinking 'I' or in any way whatever to determine it. The unity here referred to is a pure, formal, and logical unity.[9]

The Third Paralogism

The third paralogism attempts to prove that man *qua* soul is a person. The paralogism's major premise establishes what is to be understood by a person: that which at different times has consciousness of its own numerical identity. Since the soul is conscious of such a numerical identity, it is consequently a person. The major premise affirms that we are conscious of our own identity: that I am the same now as I was before—the same in the sense of being numerically the same.

Knowledge requires an "I think," i.e., it requires a consciousness for which consciousness of itself is at every moment possible. Without being able to regard the contents of consciousness as belonging to one and the same consciousness, we would not be able to speak of knowledge. But this formal, logical condition of knowledge has nothing to do with the existence of a soul that is numerically identical with itself. Even if we cannot know anything without employing the con-

[8] "Here again, as in the former paralogism, the formal proposition of apperception, 'I think,' remains the sole ground to which rational psychology can appeal when it thus ventures upon an extension of its knowledge. This proportion, however, is not itself an experience, but the form of apperception, which belongs to and precedes every experience" (A 354).

[9] "Thus the renowned psychological proof is founded merely on the indivisible unity of a representation, which governs only the verb in its relation to a person. It is obvious that in attaching 'I' to our thoughts we designate the subject of inherence only transcendentally, without noting in it any quality whatsoever—in fact, without knowing anything of it either by direct acquaintance or otherwise" (A 355).

cept 'substance,' it does not follow that we therefore must also apply the concept 'substance' to the contents of consciousness; for as Kant maintains in his *Widerlegung des Idealismus,* it is the application of the concept 'substance' to the objects of the outer world that makes possible our having knowledge of our own consciousness. The unity of self-consciousness is not, Kant maintains, a refutation of Heraclitus's teaching that everything in the world is in flux (cf. A 364).

In order to show that the unity of self-consciousness would not necessarily be at variance with the supposition of several soul substances that succeed one another, Kant gives the following illustration. An elastic ball that strikes a second similar ball transfers to this second ball its own motion and state. We can now by analogy imagine substances with representations and consciousness where one substance transfers its representations and consciousness to a second. This second substance in turn transfers its representations and consciousness (in which, of course, the first substance's representations and consciousness are included) to a third substance, and so on. The last substance will then not only have its own consciousness but in addition the consciousness of all the other substances—but have them as its own. This last substance would consequently draw an erroneous conclusion if from its own self-consciousness it were to argue to a numerically identical soul or person.

The Fourth Paralogism

The fourth paralogism is not, like the other paralogisms, concerned with the soul's existence or essence but with the existence of external objects. The paralogism reads: The existence of that which can only be inferred as a cause of given sense perceptions is subject to doubt. The existence of all outer appearances (*äusseren Erscheinungen*) is not immediately observed but is something we infer as the cause of what is sensed. The existence of all external objects is therefore doubtful.

Against this Kant maintains that external objects are not something we infer but something we directly observe, hence their existence cannot be questioned.[10] In order to support this assertion he emphasizes and elucidates the distinction between transcendental idealism and empirical realism, on the one hand, and transcendental realism and empirical idealism, on the other, a distinction we have already met in the Aesthetic. Kant declares for the transcendental idealist and the empirical realist. He thinks that the paralogism rests on a transcendental realism and an empirical idealism. To be a transcendental idealist is to deny that there are objects that do not appear in space and time; in other words, it is to deny that there are two kinds of objects: real objects (things-in-themselves) that are transcendent, and empirical objects, which are sense impressions or representations that are the effects of the transcendent objects. To be a transcendental idealist is therefore to deny what the transcendental realist maintains, for the transcendental realist holds that external objects are not sensed immediately, but rather that we sense those impressions or representations that these external (transcendent) objects produce in us. The transcendental realist is therefore necessarily an empirical idealist. The transcendental idealist, on the other hand, is an empirical realist. For him (and this can thus also be said of Kant) the empirically intuited is simply external objects.

Psychologists who are empirical idealists are also, Kant be-

[10] "All outer perception, therefore, yields immediate proof of something real in space, or rather is the real itself. In this sense empirical realism is beyond question; that is, there corresponds to our outer intuitions something real in space" (A 375).

lieves, transcendental realists and therefore susceptible to the fourth paralogism.[11]

It is important to note that Kant distinguishes between two meanings of the word 'outer' (*ausser uns*): an empirical and a transcendent meaning. According to the empirical meaning of the word, the outer is that which is in space; it is therefore that to which the categories are applicable. According to the transcendent meaning of the word, the outer is that which is independent of and unrelated to sensation. It is clear that the transcendent meaning of the word cannot be explained by reference to space. An outer object in the transcendent meaning cannot be an object that is outer in the sense that space is outside of (or inside of) me. In the empirical meaning of the word 'outer' the empirical is of course in space, and external objects are established directly. Only the word's empirical meaning is relevant when we are speaking about the existence of external objects.[12] When at certain places Kant speaks of space being in us,[13] it is clear that he can mean this

[11] "Since, so far as I know, all psychologists who adopt empirical idealism are transcendental realists, they have certainly proceeded quite consistently in ascribing great importance to empirical idealism, as one of the problems in regard to which the human mind is quite at a loss how to proceed. For if we regard outer appearances as representations produced in us by their objects, and if these objects be things existing in themselves outside us, it is indeed impossible to see how we can come to know the existence of the objects otherwise than by inference from the effect to the cause; and this being so, it must always remain doubtful whether the cause in question be in us or outside us" (A 372).

[12] "The expression 'outside us' is thus unavoidably ambiguous in meaning, sometimes signifying what as *thing in itself* exists apart from us, and sometimes what belongs solely to outer *appearance*. In order, therefore, to make this concept, in the latter sense—the sense in which the psychological question as to the reality of our outer intuition has to be understood—quite unambiguous, we shall distinguish *empirically external* objects from those which may be said to be external in the transcendental sense, by explicitly entitling the former '*things which are to be found in space*' " (A 373).

[13] See, for example, A 370, A 373, and A 375.

only in the transcendent sense of the expression 'in us.' Space is obviously not in us in the same sense that my brain is in me, but the table at which I am sitting is outside of me. If it is understood empirically, it becomes just as meaningless as saying that space is not in space.

In accordance with his empirical realism and transcendental idealism Kant rejects what he calls a transcendental dualism and therefore also a transcendental theory of perception. He rejects the supposition of a transcendent object that acts on a transcendent ego, so that what is given in space and time is its effect.[14] The difficulties connected with this problem are due to a transcendental realistic and transcendental dualistic point of view. For about the transcendent we cannot, and hence should not, speak. If as an empirical idealist one speaks only about the ideas and representations of consciousness, it would be quite without meaning to say that these ideas are external causes. If on the other hand one is a transcendental idealist and an empirical realist, the way of presenting the problem is different. External objects are neither transcendent nor empirical ideas (ideas in consciousness). The difficulties of a transcendental dualism lie, according to Kant, in the fact that it assumes a causal relationship between two such heterogeneous elements as transcendent objects and empirical ideas. For Kant this turns out to be relations between *Erscheinungen.*[15]

[14] That Kant accepts such a view is nonetheless maintained by many interpreters: cf., e.g., Adickes, *Kant und das Ding an sich;* N. Kemp Smith, *A Commentary on Kant's Critique of Pure Reason* (New York: Humanities Press, 2nd ed. rev. 1962); and Thomas D. Weldon, *Kant's Critique of Pure Reason* (2nd ed.; New York: Oxford University Press, 1958). That the views of Adickes, Smith, and Weldon are mistaken is claimed by Graham Bird, cf. his *Kant's Theory of Knowledge* (New York: Humanities Press, 1962), p. 36 ff.

[15] "As long as we take inner and outer appearances together as mere

THE ANTINOMIES OF PURE REASON

While the categorical syllogism underlies the transcendental paralogisms, the hypothetical form of inference provides the basis for the cosmological ideas.

The peculiar thing about these ideas is that when reason out of its own nature necessarily seeks the unconditioned, it appears unable to avoid arriving at two views that are in direct contradiction with each other. Reason appears, in other words, to contain antinomies; it seems to be dialectical and in conflict with itself. It arrives at the thesis with the same necessity that requires it inexorably to argue to the antithesis. According to Kant there are four such antinomies.[16]

---

representations in experience, we find nothing absurd and strange in the association of the two kinds of senses" (A 386). And later on: "The doctrine of physical influence, in its ordinary form, is, however, subject to a well-founded *critical* objection. The alleged communion between two kinds of substances, the thinking and the extended, rests on a crude dualism, and treats the extended substances, which are really nothing but mere representations of the thinking subject, as existing by themselves. This mistaken interpretation of physical influence can thus be effectively disposed of: we have shown that the proof of it is void and illicit. The much-discussed question of the communion between the thinking and the extended, if we leave aside all that is merely fictitious, comes then simply to this: *how in a thinking subject outer intuition,* namely, that of space, with its filling-in of shape and motion, *is possible*" (A 392 f.).

[16] In a letter to Professor Christian Garve, September 21, 1798, Kant writes: "As I cursorily perused your book, I came across your note on page 339, with regard to which I must lodge a protest. The point from which I started was not the inquiry about existence of God, Immortality &c. *It was the Antinomies.* The world has a beginning, it has no beginning, and so on to the fourth: there is freedom in man, there is no freedom. It was they that *awakened me from my dogmatic slumber* and drove me to a critique of our Reason, in order to remove the scandal of an apparent contradiction of Reason with itself." Of the antinomies' centrality in Kant's epistemology one gets further evidence in a letter to Marcus Hertz, dated May 11, 1781, in which Kant writes in part: "This kind of investigation will always remain difficult, and sometimes I harbour a scheme in my mind as to how it might also gain popularity. To at-

The First Antinomy

The thesis and antithesis of the first antinomy are the following: Thesis: The world has a beginning in time and is limited in space. Antithesis: The world has no beginning in time and is not limited in space.

The train of thought that Kant thinks necessarily leads to the thesis is as follows: Let us suppose that the world had no beginning in time but had always existed. Regardless of how far we were to go back in time we could never find a point where it would not be correct to say that the world had existed for an infinite time. To any moment whatever, regardless of whether it is in the infinitely remote past or the far distant future, there will thus always be added an infinite number of moments of time. What characterizes the infinite is that it is uncompleted; manifestly we can never be finished counting an infinite number. But if in order to reach the moment in which I actually now find myself time must have run through all earlier moments, then it would have run through an infinite number of moments. This clearly is impossible. Since an infinite number of moments can never be completed, it is therefore impossible that the world has always existed. The world has, therefore, a beginning in time.

That the world is limited with respect to spatial extension Kant argues for in the following way: Suppose that it were not. Considered as a whole, the world must thus be an infinitely extended magnitude. As such it would consequently

---

tempt that right at the start, when the ground had first to be cleared, would have been improper. Otherwise I should have started with the chapter on the antinomies, which might have been done in a very flourishing style and would have roused the reader's desire to investigate the sources of this conflict. But first the claims of the School must be satisfied, later one may try to please the world" (Gabriele Rabel, *Kant* [Oxford: The Clarendon Press, 1963], p. 127.

have to consist of an infinite number of simultaneously existing things. According to the axioms of intuition[17] we are only able to imagine a magnitude if we assume that it is composed of component parts.[18] This is a necessary presupposition for understanding any magnitude. As was pointed out in the discussion of the axioms of intuition, this must not be understood psychologically. It is neither true nor relevant that I am unable to picture in my mind a magnitude without first picturing it as being formed by adding one component to another. The situation must be understood logically: that the component parts of any magnitude, viewed logically, precede their being compounded into the given thing. Whatever components I may by analysis find that a thing consists of, it is still unthinkable that we should first have the thing and then thereafter its component parts. The concept 'component' has logical priority over that of which it is a component. In Kant's terminology this is expressed by saying that every magnitude is a synthesis of its components. It must be a logical possibility to imagine a thing composed of its components. But, Kant maintains, this would be excluded were there an infinite number of components. The concept of a magnitude extended infinitely in space is consequently unthinkable, which is to say that the world is limited.

The antithesis reads as follows: The world has no beginning in time and no limit in space. It is infinite both with respect to time and space. Kant's proof reads thus: Assume that it were not the case and that the world had a beginning in time. There must then have been a point in time where there was

[17] Cf. p. 77 ff.

[18] "I entitle a magnitude extensive when the representation of the parts makes possible, and therefore necessarily precedes, the representation of the whole" (B 203).

nothing. But out of nothing nothing can come. In what Kant calls empty time, i.e., a time where nothing exists and nothing happens, there is nothing that characterizes one point of time in preference to another. Every single moment is like every other moment. Therefore there can be nothing whatever that could have determined that the world should begin to exist at some particular moment. Why just this moment instead of any other? There is nothing that can distinguish or characterize that particular moment at which the world's existence is presumed to have begun. It cannot in any way be distinguished from the infinitely many other moments that did not determine the world's beginning. The world has therefore no beginning in time; it must in this respect be infinite.

Suppose next that the world were limited in space. The world would consequently have boundaries on the other side of which there would be nothing but empty space. If the world were limited, then we would necessarily have to say that it had a certain relationship to that which limited it and to whatever lay on the other side of these boundaries. For an island in the sea, for example, we can indicate the direction and distance to every point in the sea, and there is thus a relation between the island and the sea. But no such thing would be true of the world and the empty space that, on this hypothesis, would limit it. While the sea and the island are on the same logical level, this is not the case with empty space and the world. Space is a form of intuition by means of which we are able to say that different things are to be found at definite places; but space itself is not to be found at any place. This makes all talk about the relation between the world and a surrounding empty space meaningless. Therefore the world cannot be limited in space.

The Second Antinomy

The second antinomy is concerned with a thing (a substance) and the parts of which it is composed. There seem to be two possibilities: either we reach back to parts that are simple and so cannot be divided, or we never reach to such simple and indivisible parts. These two possibilities are set forth respectively in the thesis and the antithesis.

The thesis maintains that every compound substance (thing) consists of parts that are themselves indivisible. It is of these indivisible parts that the world consists, and beside them nothing else exists. Kant's proof is the following: Let us assume that composite substances were not made up of indivisible parts. If we now imagine compound substances dissolved into their parts, these parts would necessarily be simple, for otherwise there would not be anything at all remaining. If, for example, I take a machine apart, I will get a pile of screws, nuts, springs, and so on. It is possible for me to regard these as the simple parts of which the machine consists. But I can also consider each of these parts as something that itself is composed of smaller parts, of just as many parts as each part can be divided into, and every extended thing is infinitely divisible. The parts of which the substance is compounded crumble, as it were, between my fingers. They turn to nothing; nothing at all is left. It is therefore necessary to assume that a substance is composed of simple, i.e., indivisible, parts.

The antithesis maintains that no compound thing consists of simple parts, and nothing at all can be found that is simple. Let us suppose that there were things composed of simple parts. These simple, indivisible parts must necessarily be spatially extended, for a compounding of unextended parts could never yield an extended thing. But everything which is extended is divisible and therefore not simple. Regardless of how far we continue the process of dividing something extended, we can never come to something unextended.

The antithesis, which asserts that nothing at all can be found that is simple, Kant establishes by pointing out that the simple (the indivisible) never can be confirmed by experience, and even if something simple could appear in intuition, one could not justifiably conclude that something simple therefore actually existed. From the intuition of the simple we have no right, according to Kant, to infer its existence.

The Third Antinomy

The thesis maintains that causality that is in accordance with the laws of nature is not the only form of causality. We must also assume a second form of causality, namely freedom. Let us suppose that there existed only the first kind of causality. According to this, every event presupposes a preceding cause. This cause can itself only be explained, however, when it is considered to be the effect of a preceding cause, and so on. But according to this principle we can never arrive at a first cause. There cannot be any beginning to the causal sequence, which is therefore unfinished and incomplete; consequently it cannot constitute a sufficient condition for a causal explanation in accordance with the laws of nature. It is therefore necessary to assume the existence of a cause that is not itself the cause of a preceding cause. Such a cause reflects an absolute spontaneity, and this spontaneity Kant calls transcendental freedom.

The antithesis maintains that there is no freedom, and that everything that happens in the world, happens in accordance with the laws of nature. Let us suppose that this were not the case. In other words let us suppose that there is a transcendental freedom (an absolute spontaneity), that initiates a causal sequence without itself being the cause of some preceding event. The causal sequence is initiated at a definite point in time, which follows directly after another point in time. That which happens at the moment when the causal sequence begins is, however, wholly independent of that which happens (or does not happen) in the immediately preceding moment; it is not determined by this. But this conclusion contradicts the second analogy, in which Kant thinks that he has proved that every event is determined by another event directly preceding it, according to a rule. Transcendental freedom can therefore have no validity.

The Fourth Antinomy

The thesis maintains that there is a being that necessarily exists either as a part of the world or as its cause. The antithesis denies that such a being can exist.

For the thesis Kant argues in the following way: The world of experience is a world of change. A change is explained only if it is seen as caused by a preceding change, which itself must be explained as the effect of another change, and so on. Every change thus presupposes a series of changes, all of which must be seen as its conditions. But if this series is not completed, then the series that is the condition of the existence of anything at all that happens, is not completed. That such a series should be uncompleted would be (according to Kant's argument) just as catastrophic logically as though we were to suppose that an echo was an echo of a second echo, and that this echo was an echo of a third, and so on *ad infinitum*, in which case we would never have an echo that was an echo of something that was not itself an echo.[19] The series of conditions must be completed. This can only be the case if there is something that is itself not the condition of something else, which is to say, something that is unconditioned, i.e., something that exists by virtue of itself and therefore exists necessarily. Now this necessary existence, this unconditioned condition of all things, is itself a part of the world of experience. For as first cause it must precede its effect; it can only be thought of as existing in time and therefore necessarily also in the world of experience.

In the antithesis it is maintained that an absolutely necessary existing being can be neither a part of the world nor its cause. Let us suppose that there were such a necessary being. There are then two possibilities. Either it exists in the world, or it exists outside of the world. Were it to exist in the world, there would again be two possibilities: either it is a part of the world, or it is itself the world.

If it is a part of the world, then it must be the first link in a chain of causes, i.e., it must be an uncaused cause. But since it is a part of the world, it must be in time. According to the second analogy, however, that something happens in time without being followed by something else, in accordance with the rule of cause and effect, cannot be accepted. According to the second possibility, the necessary being is thought of not as a part of the world but as the world itself, i.e., as being itself the unlimited series of causes and effects. This leads to the position that a series consisting entirely of conditioned and nonnecessary links constitutes an unconditioned and necessary existence, which is impossible. If none of the parts of the series exists necessarily, the series itself cannot possess necessity.

[19] This example is not Kant's.

The possibility that the necessary existence might exist outside of the world as its cause Kant rejects for the reason that to function as a cause it would have to exercise its activity as a cause in time. But what is in time cannot be outside of the world but must necessarily be a part of it.

In each of the foregoing four antinomies the thesis reflects what Kant calls the dogmatism of pure reason, while the antithesis is an expression of empiricism.

Interest in dogmatism, i.e., an interest in affirming the unconditioned and the existence of the necessary, and in affirming freedom, is of both a practical and a speculative nature. It is of practical interest to religion and morality, Kant thinks, to maintain that man is not subject to the coercion of nature but is free and that there is a necessary and unconditioned being that underlies the world. But it is also of speculative interest, for if reason knows the unconditioned, then and only then is it possible for it to explain everything a priori. If we know what determines everything, then we can also deduce everything. This is impossible if the antithesis is valid, for according to it nothing unconditioned exists but only an infinite series of conditions of conditions.

Empiricism, which is advanced by the antithesis, has on the other hand the advantage of always having a firm and valid foundation. The knowledge that empiricism gives is secured and tested by experience, and what cannot appear as experience cannot be accepted as knowledge. The mission of empiricism, Kant believes, is to act as a brake on the tendency of reason to lay claim to a priori knowledge of the existence of the unconditioned. It is the task of empiricism to deny reason's right to such knowledge. But empiricism becomes dogmatic and exceeds its competence when it not only denies the possibility of such knowledge but in addition denies that the existence of what reason presumes to know a priori is possible.

In the antinomies, reason is, as Kant expresses it, at variance with itself, or rather, reason is at variance with itself if the antinomies cannot be solved. A solution is therefore of the utmost importance. It is, however, not only of the utmost importance; it is also, according to Kant, possible.

The concept of the conditioned requires the concept of that which conditions. We cannot have a situation where something is conditioned unless it is conditioned by something else. What Kant calls the dialectical argument of the antinomies is based on this single conceptual truth. Where something is conditioned, everything that conditions it must certainly exist. And yet is this really the simple truth? This Kant denies. It would be so, he maintains, if the conditioned were not that which is intuited in space and time but were a thing-in-itself. But the conditioned is precisely something that is only given in space and time. To recognize what is given in time and space as something conditioned is at the same time to be faced with the task of finding that which conditions this conditioned thing. But to find such a condition is to find something that is itself conditioned, and this new condition of conditions is in turn conditioned; we can continue in this way endlessly. In noting that this series of conditions of conditions is endless, we are not saying that an endless series exists, but rather that we can continue without ever coming to a last link—in exactly the same way as we may say that a series of numbers is infinite without thereby maintaining that there exists an infinite number. We only say that we can never come to a last number.

If it were the case, *per impossibile,* that space and time were things-in-themselves, then the conditioned would not only set us a task, but the condition would also have existence. Or more exactly, if the antinomies dealt with things-in-themselves, they would have to be accepted. Both the thesis and the antithesis carry the presumption that they are treating of things-in-themselves. The solution lies, therefore, in seeing that in the antinomies what is not things-in-themselves is mistakenly assumed to be so.

The form of inference of the antinomies is this:

1. If something is given as conditioned, then the entire series of its conditions also must be given.
2. Objects of sensation are given as conditioned.

---

3. The entire series of conditions of objects of sensation must therefore also be given.

In this inference it is obvious, Kant thinks, that the concept of the conditioned does not have the same meaning in the two premises. The first premise emphasizes that it is the nature of the concept of the conditioned that it presupposes all its conditions. If the conditioned is not an object of sensation, then it cannot be thought without the series of its conditions being presupposed. But in the second premise it is expressly stated that the conditioned is sense objects, which belong under the empirical.

And when it is a matter of the empirical, i.e., of that which appears in space and time, then it is *ipso facto* a matter of a temporal succession of conditions, a temporal sequence that can be continued infinitely; for if the sequence could not be continued infinitely, then we could reach something that was both unconditioned and empirical, which is an impossibility. In the first premise, on the other hand, there is no question of a temporal sequence or of anything empirical; the premise is only an expression for a conceptual rule.[20]

The concept 'the conditions of the conditioned' is thus understood differently in the two premises. In the one it is understood as affirming the existence of the whole series of conditions; it is therefore itself unconditioned. In the other premise it is not so understood. It is not a statement about the unconditioned as something given or existing but rather a statement that must be viewed as a rule that prescribes a never-ending search after the conditions of the conditions. Therefore it prohibits us from viewing anything as being in itself unconditioned. Kant calls this a *regulative* principle. To regard the series of conditions as something given and therefore not as an infinite succession is to view them *constitutively*.

The Solution of the First Antinomy

Let us first look at the thesis, which states that the world has a beginning in time and is limited with respect to space. Now an absolute beginning or an absolute limit can never appear in experience. According to the regulative principle there is nothing that can be regarded as the absolutely last. Every experience leads to a next; the sequence of possible experi-

[20] "The synthesis of the conditioned with its conditions (and the whole series of the latter) does not in the major premiss carry with it any limitation through time or any concept of succession. The empirical synthesis, on the other hand, that is, the series of the conditions in appearance, as subsumed in the minor premiss, is necessarily successive, the members of the series being given only as following upon one another in time; and I have therefore, in this case, no right to assume the absolute *totality* of the synthesis and of the series thereby represented. In the major premiss all members of the series are given in themselves, without any condition of time, but in this minor premiss they are possible only through the successive regress, which is given only in the process in which it is actually carried out" (B 528 f.).

ences (i.e., intuition in space and time) has no last link. Therefore we cannot speak of the totality of all experiences, which we certainly could do if the world had a beginning in time and were limited in space. Since the thesis is precisely about time (the world has a beginning in time) and about space (the world is limited in space), we would not have been able to have used the regulative principle if space and time were not forms of intuition but were things-in-themselves. We would have had instead a constitutive use, which would have meant that the thesis had validity.

But the antithesis, which states that the world is infinite with respect to time and space, is not therefore correct. The world is neither finite nor infinite. It is not an infinite magnitude. But we can proceed from one point to another endlessly, which is something other than its being infinite. No straight line is infinitely long, but every straight line can be lengthened infinitely.[21]

The Solution of the Second Antinomy

The thesis maintains that a concept is composed of absolutely simple (i.e., indivisible) parts. But nothing in experience can be absolutely simple. Here too the regulative principle is in force, and it is a violation of this principle to view anything as an absolute last. But the claim of the antithesis, that no composite thing is composed of simple parts, is not right either, for no compound thing is at any moment ever divided into an infinite number of parts but only into a finite number. An infinite number is not a number at all. A cake

[21] "For the solution, therefore, of the first cosmological problem we have only to decide whether in the regress to the unconditioned magnitude of the universe, in time and space, this never limited ascent can be called a regress to infinity, or only an indeterminately continued regress (in indefinitum)" (B 546).

is in theory infinitely divisible, but at any given moment it is divided into a definite (finite) number of pieces (or perhaps not divided at all). It is nonsense to say that it has been divided into an infinite number of pieces.

The Solution of the Third Antinomy

The third antinomy maintains in its thesis that there must be a first cause that spontaneously, and as an expression of its freedom, begins of itself, while the antithesis denies that such a thing is possible. Kant will not solve this antinomy by showing that freedom is a reality or by showing that it is in any case a possibility. He will solve it by showing that freedom is not inconsistent with nature.[22] The antinomy is thus not really an antinomy but is two propositions, both of which can be true. It is correct to say, as stated by the antithesis, that everything is subject to causality and therefore there is no first cause that begins spontaneously—provided, to be sure, that we speak of what is intuited in space and time. What experience yields, and necessarily must yield, is a sequence of events in which each event is determined by the foregoing. An event that is not determined by something preceding it does not satisfy the conditions of experience. When it is a matter of what is intuited in space and time, the antithesis is correct.

But it would not be a contradiction to speak, as does the thesis, of a wholly other kind of causality, which is not in time and consequently has no beginning. This causality does determine what occurs in space and time but determines it without being itself an event, without being something

[22] "What we have alone been able to show, and what we have alone been concerned to show, is that this antinomy rests on a sheer illusion, and that causality through freedom is at least *not incompatible with* nature" (B 586).

that happens. It is a determination of what exists in time without itself being in time.

If a ball strikes a second ball, which thereby begins to roll, the impact of the first ball is the cause of the motion of the second. According to Kant we should then be able to maintain that the fact that the first ball's impact made the second ball roll is itself caused, and that this cause is not in space and time.[23] It must, however, again be stressed that Kant does not think that he has proved that such an intelligible cause exists, or that its existence is probable or merely possible. He would only maintain that there is no logical contradiction involved in such a concept. As to how such a causality is further to be understood, nothing is said, and in the nature of the case nothing can be said. For a condition of understanding is precisely the kind of causality which exists in time. A nonempirical causality could consequently never be of use in explaining anything that exists in experience. Everything that is or can be an object of experience is, according to Kant, fully explained through empirical laws.[24]

[23] "Now granting that effects are appearances and that their cause is likewise appearance, is it necessary that the causality of their cause should be exclusively empirical? May it not rather be, that while for every effect in the (field of) appearance a connection with its cause in accordance with the laws of empirical causality is indeed required, this empirical causality, without the least violation of its connection with natural causes, is itself an effect of a causality that is not empirical but intelligible? This latter causality would be the action of a cause which, in respect of appearances, is original, and therefore, as pertaining to this faculty, not appearance but intelligible; although it must otherwise, in so far as it is a link in the chain of nature, be regarded as entirely belonging to the world of sense" (B 572).

[24] "This intelligible ground does not have to be considered in empirical enquiries; it concerns only thought in the pure understanding; and although the effects of this thought and action of the pure understanding are to be met with in the appearances, these appearances must none the less be capable of complete causal explanation in terms of other appearances in accordance with natural laws. We have to take their strictly empirical character as the supreme ground of explanation, leaving entirely

Kant believes that these considerations are applicable to man. Every man's character and actions can be fully explained on the basis of empirical laws. In this respect they are causally determined. With sufficient knowledge of the relevant empirical relationships we could predict what a particular individual's actions would be in a particular situation. In this respect there is no difference between human actions and things that happen in nature. But while it would be meaningless to say of things that happen in nature that they ought to happen otherwise than as they actually do, it is obviously not meaningless to say of a man that he ought to have acted otherwise than he in fact did.

Let us consider Kant's own example. A man tells a spiteful lie. It is possible to explain this action causally: the man's heredity, his bad upbringing and associates, and many other relevant factors can serve as sufficient ground for an explanation. His action must be seen as a necessary effect of all these relationships. But in addition to establishing that the action (or the will, as Kant expresses it) is causally determined, we also make a judgment about it. We reproach him for acting as he did. He ought not to have acted in this way. Behind this reproach, behind this 'ought,' lies a nonempirical, a priori law, a law of reason, which expresses itself in an imperative. In this reproach there is entailed the notion that the man in question could have acted as he ought to have acted. His will could have been determined by the law of reason instead of by these empirical motives.

What does it mean to say that the will is determined by pure reason rather than by empirical motives? It does not

out of account their intelligible character (that is, the transcendental cause of their empirical character) as being completely unknown, save in so far as the empirical serves for its sensible sign" (B 573).

mean that these empirical motives do not manifest themselves as something that a man wants to do; it means, rather, that the agent, or more correctly (to use Kant's expression) his will, frees itself from them and obeys reason's a priori law instead. This law must be universally valid, otherwise it would not be a priori. In his chief work on ethics, *The Critique of Practical Reason,* Kant formulates this law of reason as follows: A man ought so to act that the maxim of his willing can at the same time hold as a principle of a universally valid law.[25]

Let us assume the existence of a will that in spite of contrary motives is determined by reason. It will then be determined by the special form of causality that Kant calls transcendental freedom. We are not here speaking about a certain event that occurs in space and time and is the cause of a subsequent event. It would be a misunderstanding to speak of a law as being an event—as being something that happened. A law can be a prescription for events or actions, but it is not itself an event or an action.[26] The law of reason is not itself caused or determined by anything, and it determines without itself being in space and time; whereas that to which it gives rise, occurs or begins at a definite time and at a definite place. Freedom can therefore be understood both negatively and positively. It is negative in the sense that it means a freedom from (an independence of) empirical motives, but it is positive in the sense that the law of reason is able to bring about events.[27]

[25] *Op. cit.*, p. 54.

[26] "Reason is present in all the actions of men at all times, and under all circumstances, and is always the same; but it is not itself in time, and does not fall into any new state in which it was not before. In respect to new states, it is *determining,* not *determinable*" (B 584).

[27] "This freedom ought not, therefore, to be conceived only negatively as

An action that is determined by reason is in time and space. In agreement with the second analogy it must be regarded and understood as the effect of a preceding cause operating in space and time. Regardless of what action a person may perform, whether it be an action he ought or ought not to perform, it must be explicable. This means that appropriate psychological laws will be able to indicate the feelings, motives and thoughts that explain why the person in question acted as he did. The fact that he realizes a particular action is what the law of reason demands and that this realization, in connection with what Kant calls a respect for this law, makes him act as the law of reason prescribes is not inconsistent with the assertion that the law's command (its 'ought') gives a (transcendental) determination of the agent's will.

As has been said, Kant does not believe he has demonstrated the existence of transcendental freedom, but he does think he has proved it is not inconsistent with the second analogy. Or, as he also expresses it, there is no conflict between nature and freedom.

The Solution of the Fourth Antinomy

Kant believes that the fourth antinomy can be solved in the same way as the third. The thesis and antithesis are not inconsistent with each other. The validity of the antithesis does not necessarily entail the invalidity of the thesis. They can both be valid. The antithesis is valid so far as the empirical

---

independence of empirical conditions. The faculty of reason, so regarded, would cease to be a cause of appearances. It must also be described in positive terms, as the power of originating a series of events. In reason itself nothing begins; as unconditioned condition of every voluntary act, it admits of no conditions antecedent to itself in time. Its effect has, indeed, a beginning in the series of appearances, but never in this series an absolutely first beginning" (B 581 f.).

world is concerned, but not the thesis. If the objects of the empirical world, which are objects in space and time, were instead things-in-themselves, then the thesis would be invalid. The antithesis would then be the only possible assertion, and all talk of a necessary existence would be rendered impossible. But since the antithesis holds only for the empirical world, it is only of that world that we can affirm with certainty that there can be no necessary existence. This does not exclude (but neither does it prove or make probable) that there exists a nonempirical and necessary condition of the uncompleted and uncompletable series of the empirically conditioned. However, such a condition must be found, if it can be found at all, outside of this sequence and not as a link in it.

Kant believes he has herewith solved the fourth antinomy by showing there is no conflict between thesis and antithesis. But as we have said above, he does not think he has given any argument to show the thesis is true. There is a difference between showing that the possible truth of the thesis is not in conflict with the truth of the antithesis, and showing that the thesis actually is true. The question of the truth of the thesis, which is a question as to whether an unconditioned and necessary existence can be established, leads into speculative theology and Kant's critique of it.

THE IDEAL OF PURE REASON

The Concept of God

While it is the categorical syllogism that underlies the paralogisms and the hypothetical inference that underlies the antinomies, it is the disjunctive inference that provides the basis for speculative theology.

It can be maintained of every thing that either the predicate

P or its contradictory predicate not-*P* belongs to it. Every thing must be either *P* or not-*P*, but nothing can have them both at one and the same time. A special relation obtains, however, between a certain class of predicates and the negation of these predicates. It is not simply that such pairs of predicates cannot both be ascribed to the same thing. The point is rather that one of any such a pair is a negative predicate in the sense that it negates all content and can only be understood on condition that the other predicate, the positive predicate, is also understood. Darkness is not simply the opposite of light; in order to understand what darkness is, knowledge of light is presupposed. A man born blind, Kant maintains, will not know what darkness is, for he has never seen light, and without knowing what light is, he will not know what darkness is. He who was born in poverty and has never seen anything other than poverty (Kant speaks of "the savages") does not know what poverty is, for he does not know what prosperity is; and he who is ignorant does not know what ignorance is, for he does not know what knowledge is. Of the pairs of concepts that have here been mentioned it is the predicates 'light,' 'prosperity,' and 'knowledge' that are presuppositions of the others. They reflect reality, not the lack of it. The concepts 'dark,' 'poverty,' and 'ignorance' are predicates only in the sense that they indicate the aspect of reality that is lacking. It is correct to say that the poor lack money and what money can buy, and that the ignorant lack knowledge. But it is nonsense to say that the rich are lacking in poverty and that the learned have a lack of ignorance.

Every existing thing is characterized by the predicates that apply to it. Some of these predicates will be positive, and others will be negative. If we take all possible existing predicates, then for any given predicate either that predicate or its contrary will necessarily apply. If the predicate *P* is not applicable, then the predicate not-*P* must be. The fewer the negative predicates that apply to a thing the more reality it has. But since everything that exists is finite and limited, it will therefore also have some negative predicates. And since negative predicates can only be understood through the corresponding positive predicates, then there must be an idea that is the idea of all possible positive predicates. This idea of the sum total of all conceivable, positive predicates is not understood simply as an idea but, in addition, as an existing thing; yet not as an object of experience, for whatever is found in experience is of course finite and limited, but as a thing-in-itself. It is a thing that serves as the presupposition and basis for every determination of the objects of experience. It serves therefore as an ideal, or as Kant expresses it, a transcendental ideal.[28] It is real and individual, for it is determined by all positive predicates that belong to everything real; it is a being, indeed the highest being (*ens entium*), since there can be nothing that is more real than it. The concept of such a being is the concept of God.

There is, however, a difference between maintaining that the concept of the totality of all positive properties is presupposed by the determination of various empirical objects, and then claiming that a real being, corresponding to this concept, exists.

[28] "But the concept of what thus possesses all reality is just the concept of a *thing in itself* as completely determined; and since in all possible (pairs of) contradictory predicates one predicate, namely, that which belongs to being absolutely, is to be found in its determination, the concept of an *ens realissimum* is the concept of an individual being. It is therefore a transcendental *ideal* which serves as basis for the complete determination that necessarily belongs to all that exists. This ideal is the supreme and complete material condition of the possibility of all that exists—the condition to which all thought of objects, so far as their content is concerned, has to be traced back" (B 604).

To maintain the latter, Kant thinks, is a fiction.[29] But even if it is a fiction, an illusion of reason, to maintain the existence of such a being, nonetheless men have supposed that its existence can be demonstrated by reason. Kant must therefore show that these proofs are erroneous. Only three different kinds of proofs are possible: (1) the physicotheological proof, (2) the cosmological proof, and (3) the ontological proof. Of these three proofs Kant considers the ontological to be the most essential and the most fundamental. He begins, therefore, by examining it.

The Ontological Proof of God

The ontological argument is based on the concept of necessary existence, i.e., an existence it would be impossible to deny. But what does it mean to say that something exists necessarily? What are we to understand by a being that necessarily exists? What makes the nonexistence of such a being impossible? If we cannot answer these questions, then we cannot possibly give any meaning to the concept 'a being that necessarily exists,' and according to Kant, this is precisely what we cannot do. For neither a subject nor a predicate can have necessity; only the judgments that result when certain predicates are ascribed to certain subjects can have necessity. That the sum of the angles of a triangle is 180° is a judgment that is necessarily true; but neither the triangle nor the sum of its angles is

[29] "In any such use of the transcendental idea we should, however, be overstepping the limits of its purpose and validity. For reason, in employing it as a basis for the complete determination of things, has used it only as the *concept* of all reality, without requiring that all this reality be objectively given and be itself a thing. Such a thing is a mere fiction in which we combine and realise the manifold of our idea in an ideal, as an individual being" (B 608).

necessary. The 'necessary truth' of the judgment is therefore hypothetical. This judgment simply asserts that if there is a triangle, then the sum of its angles is 180°. But the judgment that triangles exist is not a judgment that is necessarily true. We can say that should there exist a being whose existence is necessary, then its nonexistence is impossible, and it would be a contradiction to deny this. It would also be a contradiction to make the judgment: should there exist a being whose existence is necessary, then its nonexistence is possible. But it is not a contradiction to maintain that there is no being whose existence is necessary. The judgment, "God is almighty," is a necessarily true judgment; for the concept 'almighty' follows from the concept 'God.' But the judgment, "God does not exist," is not a contradiction. From the necessarily true judgment, "God is almighty," the judgment, "God exists," does not follow.[30]

Kant concludes by saying that we cannot have a concept of a being where a denial of this being's existence would be a contradiction.

But the ontological proof of God is intended as a proof that such a concept exists: The concept of a being that has all positive properties (*ens realissimum*) must also have the property 'existence,' for existence is a positive property. To deny the existence of such a being is therefore a self-contradiction. Against this argument Kant makes the following objection: If we say of a thing that it exists, what kind of judgment have we set forth? It must be either analytic or synthetic. If it is an

[30] " 'God is omnipotent' is a necessary judgment. The omnipotence cannot be rejected if we posit a Deity, that is, an infinite being; for the two concepts are identical. But if we say, 'There is no God,' neither the omnipotence nor any other of its predicates is given; they are one and all rejected together with the subject, and there is therefore not the least contradiction in such a judgment" (B 623).

analytic judgment, then the predicate contains nothing that is not already in the concept of the subject; it belongs to the concept itself in the same way in which the predicate "equilateral" belongs to the concept 'equilateral triangle.' But if this is the case, then, for example, the concept 'a golden mountain' will never be complete, so long at least as there are no golden mountains. But the concept 'a golden mountain' does not change according to whether golden mountains are or are not to be found. The assertion that something or other exists (let us call such assertions existential assertions) cannot therefore be analytic. They must consequently be synthetic. But if we get a contradiction only by denying an analytic judgment, and if existential judgments are synthetic, then to deny them can never involve us in a contradiction.

Furthermore, existence is not at all what Kant calls a real predicate, one, that is, that adds some property to a subject. The difference between the propositions (1) "God is almighty" and (2) "God exists" is evident. In (1) a certain property is predicated of God, namely, the property of being almighty; in (2), however, no property is predicated of God.[31] A debate about God's omnipotence is one about what properties belong to God; but a debate about God's existence is not such a debate. It is a debate about whether the concept 'God,' with

[31] A comparison of Kant and Russell with respect to the concept of existence is not without interest. Like Kant, Russell maintains that in the proposition, "God exists," 'exists' is not a predicate. But in addition Russell argues that 'God' in the above proposition is not a name (a subject) but is what Russell calls a propositional function. The difference is expressed briefly but precisely in the following statement of Ryle: "Since Kant, we have, most of us, paid lip service to the doctrine that 'existence is not a quality' and so we have rejected the pseudo-implication of the ontological argument. . . . But until fairly recently it was not noticed that if in 'God exists' 'exists' is not a predicate (save in grammar), then in the same statement 'God' cannot be (save in grammar) the subject of predication" ("Systematically misleading expressions," in *Logic and Language*, First Series, ed. A. G. N. Flew [Oxford: Blackwell, 1951]).

the properties that we think ought to belong to this concept, corresponds to something actual. As Kant understands the ontological proof of God, it rests upon the presupposition that existence is a positive property of *ens realissimum*, and he believes that he has already shown this proposition to be erroneous.[32]

The Cosmological Proof

Kant formulates the cosmological proof thus: If anything exists, then an absolutely necessary being also exists. Now I, at least, exist; therefore an absolutely necessary being exists.

The structure of the proof is related to the thesis of the fourth antinomy: In the world of experience everything that happens is caused by something that precedes it, and this again is caused by some third thing, and so on. Everything is conditioned by something else. But the series of conditions presupposes the unconditioned, which means an unconditioned condition that necessarily exists. And this necessarily existing condition possesses the highest form of reality: it is *ens realissimum*. According to Kant this proof presupposes the ontological proof, because the proof includes the assertion that what exists necessarily possesses the highest form of reality, a form that is not limited in any way whatever. Kant shows this in the following manner: The proposition, "That which exists necessarily possesses the highest form of reality," can be converted *per accidens;* we then obtain the proposition, "Some

[32] The ontological proof for God has quite recently been an object of renewed interest. Here only two essays will be mentioned: S. A. Grave, "The Ontological Argument of St. Anselm," *Philosophy*, XXVII, No. 100 (1952); Norman Malcolm, "Anselm's Ontological Argument," *The Philosophical Review*, LXIX (1962), pp. 41–62 (reprinted in Norman Malcolm, *Knowledge and Certainty* [Englewood Cliffs, N.J.: Prentice-Hall, 1963], pp. 141–63).

things that possess the highest form of reality exist necessarily." But since all things that possess the highest form of reality are identical—they have, of course, exactly the same properties—the converted proposition holds for everything that possesses the highest form of reality. This last proposition is based on the pattern of thought of the ontological proof. *Ens realissimum* contains necessarily the property "existence" and consequently necessarily exists. Since the cosmological proof presupposes the ontological, which Kant has just shown to be invalid, it follows that the cosmological proof is likewise invalid.

Moreover we find in the proof the error that is characteristic of the transcendental dialectic: what has validity (or at least meaning) only in experience is applied transcendently. It is only within experience that we can infer a preceding cause from something that happens. But to argue to a cause that lies outside of space and time is, according to Kant, meaningless. Ideas viewed as regulative require us to proceed from a given cause to *its* cause and so on *ad infinitum,* and to proceed from something conditioned to *its* condition and, further, to this latter condition's own condition; but they forbid us to infer a first cause and an unconditioned condition. Everything that exists can also be thought of as not existing, and its existence, therefore, is not necessary. We can, however, have conditions that are necessary for a thing's existence, and these conditions, again, have conditions. This series of conditions can never be completed. We can therefore never, as the cosmological proof assumes that we can, *begin* with a necessary existence.

The Physicotheological Proof

This proof is based on the regularity of nature, which is thought to be a fact. We find that the processes of nature are directed toward ends; they are instrumental. They are as they are because only thereby can nature's various ends be reached. Such regularity and purposefulness can only be the result of an intelligence that exists outside of nature. We conclude, therefore, that the course of nature, which is so regular and purposeful, is due to an almighty, all-knowing, and necessarily existing being.

But even if we admit that the processes of nature proceed purposefully, this does not entitle us, Kant maintains, to argue to a creator of the world but at most to a cosmic master builder.

With respect to the properties that such a world builder must possess, we are only entitled to conclude that he must be wise and mighty, not that he is all-wise and almighty.[33] The leap from being wise and mighty to being all-wise and almighty—i.e., to being perfect,[34] or, in other words, to being *ens realissimum*—the physicotheological proof cannot justify. The leap presupposes the cosmological and therefore also the ontological proofs. And since the ontological proof, which is presupposed by both of the two other proofs and is therefore the fundamental proof, depends upon a logical error, it follows that none of the three proofs of the existence of God is valid. It is impossible by means of reason to prove God's existence, but it is also, according to Kant, impossible to refute it.

[33] "Now no one, I trust, will be so bold as to profess that he comprehends the relation of the magnitude of the world as he has observed it (alike as regards both extent and content) to omnipotence, of the world order to supreme wisdom, of the world unity to the absolute unity of its Author, etc." (B 656).

[34] "But since we cannot, as regards causality, dispense with an ultimate and supreme being, what is there to prevent us ascribing to it a degree of perfection that sets it *above everything else that is possible?*" (B 651).

THE REGULATIVE USE OF THE IDEAS

We have seen that the ideas of reason lead to metaphysical illusions. The ideas as such are not erroneous; it is the manner of their employment that leads to the error. As mentioned earlier, they can be used either constitutively or regulatively. If they are used constitutively, the result is a metaphysical illusion; if they are used regulatively, they are not only useful but also indispensable. In the constitutive use we let the idea stand for an object, albeit a transcendent object, that lies beyond what it is possible to experience, to think, to understand, and to connect something with. We think and understand by means of categories, and categories can only be employed in experience. The constitutive use results in the claim that the soul, the world as a totality, and God exist. This means also the existence of the absolute, the unconditioned, and the necessary. The illusions, which are the result of the constitutive use of reason, have been clarified, as we have seen, in the paralogisms, the antinomies, and speculative theology. Thc goal of the regulative use of the ideas, on the other hand, is to bring the greatest possible unity into our knowledge. To attempt to bring such unity into knowledge is a logical principle; it is a necessary law of reason. For without this law there would be no reason, and without reason no coherent use of the understanding, and therefore no criterion of empirical truth either.[35]

[35] "The law of reason which requires us to seek for this unity, is a necessary law, since without it we should have no reason at all, and without reason no coherent employment of the understanding, and in the absence of this no sufficient criterion of empirical truth. In order, therefore, to secure an empirical criterion we have no option save to presuppose the systematic unity of nature as objectively valid and necessary" (B 679).

While the constitutive use of the idea asserts the existence of a transcendent object corresponding to the idea, the significance of the regulative idea lies in its being that which gives direction to knowledge. Knowledge proceeds *as if* there were such objects, which it was the goal of knowledge to know. The progress of knowledge is a never-ending process toward this goal, this ideal.

Psychological research aims at finding an ever-expanding unity among the many different phenomena and manifestations of consciousness. The ideal striven for (but never reached) is the idea of a soul-substance that remains unchanged while the different states of consciousness are in ceaseless flux. To aim at such a unity is the essence of knowledge. In order to have psychological knowledge we must proceed *as if* there were such a substance. This "as if" is not the "as if" that we find, for example, in the assertion, "He acts as if he were a millionaire (which he is not)," but rather the 'as if' of possibility, as in the assertion, "He acts as if he were a millionaire (which he may perhaps be)." But we have no logical right, according to Kant, to deny that there are such objects as a soul and God; we must simply recognize that all attempts by reason to reach a knowledge of their existence are doomed in advance.[36] And from the fact that we have no logical right to deny their existence it is a considerable leap to assume their existence. Indeed, the leap is so great that Kant denies that we are entitled to make it. As a regulative idea, it is not dependent upon

[36] "Now there is nothing whatsoever to hinder us from *assuming* these ideas to be also objective, that is, from hypostatising them—except in the case of the cosmological ideas, where reason, in so proceeding, falls into antinomy. The psychological and theological ideas contain no antinomy, and involve no contradiction. How, then, can anyone dispute their (possible) objective reality? He who denies their possibility must do so with just as little knowledge (of this possibility) as we can have in affirming it" (B 701).

whether there actually exists a transcendent object corresponding to the idea. To conceive of the idea as regulative is to conceive of it as a rule that requires us always to seek after greater unity and never to assume that this unity has been reached.

In cosmology, according to the regulative meaning of the idea, we should always attempt to find every condition's condition. Scientific endeavor ought to proceed as if it were directed toward finding an unconditioned or first condition. But the idea would miss its regulative meaning and instead become constitutive if at any given moment or at any particular point in scientific development we were to regard something as the unconditioned. Experience can never become a completed sequence of events; for the world as something completed, i.e., as a totality, is an illusion that results from the idea having been used constitutively. Experience can never disclose an unconditioned and necessary first link nor an absolutely last link.

If we assume a necessarily existing being, which has created the world according to a definite plan, then we have used the theological idea constitutively. To use the idea regulatively means that in the exploration of nature we proceed as if everything in nature had a definite function. In the study of an organism, for example, we will be guided by the principle that the organism has a definite function to fulfill and that it functions as it does because a particular result is thereby best attained. Thus understood and used, the idea does not give rise to the supposition of the existence of something lying *outside* of experience. Its function is to better organize and understand what lies *within* experience.

5) Conclusion

Kant formulates his central problem as the problem of how synthetic a priori judgments are possible. The problem is not whether there are such judgments, for Kant thinks that he can easily show that there are. That judgments of mathematics and certain stated principles of natural science are both synthetic and a priori is not for him a problem. The argumentation for this view is already to be found in the introduction and appears to give him neither misgivings nor difficulties. If we view *The Critique of Pure Reason* from this way of presenting the problem, we find his solution to be that the propositions of mathematics are synthetic a priori because space and time are a priori forms of intuition; and that the principles of pure natural science are synthetic a priori because the categories of the understanding are necessary presuppositions of all understanding; and finally that in metaphysics we can make no synthetic a priori judgments. Metaphysics is a transcendental illusion.

There is, however, a disadvantage to this way of characterizing Kant's *Critique of Pure Reason,* namely, that it rests on the supposition of synthetic a priori judgments. The validity of *The Critique of Pure Reason* would thereby depend on the validity of this supposition. The question as to how synthetic a priori judgments are possible becomes at best irrelevant if there are no such judgments. And the fact is that the period after Kant has been by no means in general agreement with him on just this question. In our century the logical positivists, among others, have argued cogently against the existence of such judgments, though today we are by no means as certain about this as were (and are) the logical positivists. The problem is under continuing debate, and it has proved (one is tempted to add, 'of course') to be more complicated than either Kant or the logical positivists anticipated.

One of philosophy's most famous works cannot, however, stand or fall with the result that might possibly be arrived at respecting this particular question. There are other and more fruitful ways in which to consider *The Critique of Pure Reason.* For it is entirely correct to regard this work as a profound, sometimes revolutionary, examination of a number of fundamental philosophical problems and not just as an attempt to answer a single question. Whether or not Kant has solved these various problems (which he certainly has not) is by no means decisive for evaluating the worth and relevance of the *Critique.* The important thing is that he has been able to throw so much philosophical light over so many of our fundamental concepts that we can now view them (and thereby many of the philosophical problems connected with these concepts) from an enriched perspective. There is a decisive difference in philosophy before and after Kant.

What Kant says about space and time in the Transcendental Aesthetic is not final, but certain of their fundamental features and certain fundamental distinctions between them and concepts such as 'thing' and 'event' are of epoch-making significance.

More clearly and more profoundly than anyone else, Kant has recognized that experience involves the use of concepts. Certain concepts exist whose existence is not the *result* of experience but on the contrary the *condition* of it—an insight that in our day is making more and more progress.

Kant's idea that the categories are a condition of experience is a blow against that form of empiricism—sensationism—for which Hume made himself a spokesman and which he carried through to the bitter end. Against this form of empiricism, which seems to lead to the impossibility of all knowledge, Kant has given if not a final or universally accepted argument, still one that is profound.

Kant opposes the Humean form of empiricism at the same time as he emphasizes that knowledge is only given in experience. He attains thereby to a deeper understanding of the concept of experience. Not least, through his view of the concept 'experience,' Kant has contributed to the development of the theory of knowledge. It is an advance from a pre-philosophical view of this concept to one characterized by the greatest philosophical insight. The increased philosophical interest in the logic of language, and thereby in those concepts that are the condition of language and of its rules, is in a certain sense Kantian. It is in many respects contrary to philosophy that bears the stamp of Hume.

Kant's antimetaphysical attitude is a consequence of his concept of experience. For the categories, which are necessary conditions of experience, are empty without intuition. If one does violence to this principle, the result is transcendental illusions.

In his denial of metaphysics Kant is in line with the logical positivists and with many other modern philosophers as well. And yet there is a decisive difference between Kant and the logical positivists. For the logical positivists consider metaphysical assertions to be meaningless; such assertions, they argue, are actually not assertions at all but pseudo-assertions, and as such they are neither true nor false. For Kant metaphysical assertions are without epistemological value. But even though we have no right to assume the existence of metaphysical objects, neither do we have the right to deny them. Consistent with this view, Kant in his ethics (in *The Critique of Practical Reason*) thinks that we are able to postulate freedom, the immortality of the soul, and the existence of God.

When I said above that many modern philosophers reject metaphysics, this must be taken with a certain reservation. For by metaphysics we are inclined today to mean not only (or perhaps not at all) philosophizing about God, the world and the soul but rather philosophizing about such fundamental concepts as space, time, existence, and many others. In this understanding of the word 'metaphysics' *The Critique of Pure Reason* is a model of metaphysical investigation.

Whether or not one is in agreement with the arguments of *The Critique of Pure Reason*, it would indicate a deficient understanding of philosophical thought if one were not to view it with deepest respect. To read this work is to follow one of mankind's most gifted persons in his effort to reach clarity about the most difficult problems of thought. To have the opportunity to take part in this endeavor and, according to the best of one's abilities, to comprehend the power of his thought, is one of the richest experiences that a man can be granted.